Maha Dasoha Sutras

By

Poojya Dr. Sharnbasvappa Appa
Mahadasoha Peethadhipathi
Shri Sharnbasveshwar Samsthan, Gulbarga
Karnataka State – India

TRANSLATION AND COMMENTARY

By

Sri. M.V. Kamath
Chairman
Prasara Barathi
Government of India (INDIA)

SERIALS PUBLICATIONS
NEW DELHI (INDIA)

Mahadasoha Sutras by Poojya Dr. Sharnbasvappa Appa, Translation and Commentary by Sri. M.V. Kamath, Journalist.

First Published - 2006

ISBN : 81-8387-045-7

Published by

SERIALS PUBLICATIONS
4830/24, Prahlad Street, Ansari Road
Darya Ganj, New Delhi-110002 (India)
Phone: 23245225. Fax: 91-11-23272135
E-mail: serials@satyam.net.in

Poojya Dr. Sharanbasawappa Appa

ABOUT POOJYA APPAJI

I consider it as matter of grate honour to introduce Poojya Dr. Sharnbasvappa Appaji, a great Philosopher, a poet, a great educationist, a Social reformer and above all a great humanist.

Born into an illustrious family on 14th November, 1935 Appaji became an heir to the Piety that runs in the family, as his dedication to the Service of man and God amply demonstrates. Educated at one of the leading Universities in India *i.e.*, Karnataka University, Dharwad, and did his Post Graduation in Philosophy. Appaji began his distinguished and manifold career as a member of the Syndicate of the Karnataka University, before emerging as pioneer in the field of education. A number of institutions, including the university of Gulbarga, bear witness to his passionate commitment to the cause of education and progressive outlook, by opening the doors to the latest disciplines, including Computer Science, Electronics, Business Management, and P.G. Course in Fine Arts.

By establishing residential school which runs on the Public School Model, Appaji provides the most scientific and modern form of education from Montessori to Post Graduate Level. Truly, it was Appaji who put Gulbarga on the map of education in India.

The educational institutions founded by Appaji Propound, like the Shantiniketan, a Philosophy that is not only a cardinal Principle of his creed but can also serve as an answer to the present day malaise. Education, far from being a mere means to livelihood, must be harnessed to the service of man in the true spirit of Kayaka and Dasoha.

Hence the introduction in some of these institutions "Earn while you Learn" Schemes which are in tune with the current demand for the right to work as a fundamental right.

Appaji has distinguished himself as an administrator Par Excellence, in recognition of which he was unanimously elected as a President of the Hyderabad Karnataka Education Society, and the most Modern Basaveshwara Hospital in Gulbarga owes its existence to his vision, and he has held several positions with great distinction.

Poojya Dr. Sharnbasvappa Appa sands as an exemplary of secular and universal instincts of man. The composition of 21 Mahadasoha Sutras, which have won international acclaim by writers like Judith Kroll, is a testimonial to his gracious nobility. By the grace of Poojya Appaji's divine vision and direction, the Sangha has developed into a magnificent educational complex. The Dasoha Philosophy is Institutionalized in the vision of the sangha that endeavors to attain excellence in service as reflected in these words by Poojya Dr. Sharnbasvappa Appa. *"No Religion is greater than service and service to humanity is service to God"*, *"Teaching and learning for the sake of livelihood is an ordinary life. Teaching and learning not only for the sake of livelihood but also for the welfare of others is a good cultured life. Teaching and learning not only for the sake of livelihood but for the sake of the welfare of humanity, thinking that serving humanity is serving God, is Kayaka and Dasoha Philosophy of Education"*. It should be noted here that culture gives while vulture snatches. Thus culture is humane and vulture is barbarous.

Shri Sharnbasveshwar Vidya Vardhak Sangha today runs 45 educational Institutions, imparting education to 16000 students which includes 10000 boys and 6000 girls. The Institutions range from Montessori to Post Graduation in Arts, Science, Commerce, B.B.M., M.B.A., B.C.A., M.C.A., D.Ed., AND B.Ed., Engineering and Public Schools. During the 100 years of service, the Sangha has invested Rs. 100 crores for the benefit of the students and many more educational proposals are on the cards. And centenary celebration of Sangha was also inaugurated by the Honourable President Dr. A.P.J. Abdul Kalam.

The Sangha is the pioneer to start PG Course in Fine Arts and Music in the whole of South Indian in 1982 much before the Government and University could conceive this idea.

Sharnbasveshwar Public School one among 68 Public Schools of India proudly stands as a beacon light for many aspiring *young* students of this region who crave for an education of *International* Standards. The motto of the Institution–"Discipline, Excellence, Hard work and Service. We offer *education* to our students, to overcome many challenges. *Think Independently, Write Independently, speak Independently, Live Independently* to face the challenges in the life to serve, not only his family, but also whole National-Mankind.

In appreciation of the manifold services of the Appaji who has traversed vast grounds in the Propagation of Dasoha and the oneness of man, Gulbarga University, Gulbarga conferred Honorary Doctorate Degree on Poojya Sharnbasvappa Appaji.

The Dasoha Principles propagated by Appaji have divested themselves of all sectarian elements and became great Universal Principles.

Just as Yoga developed into Poorna Yoga in Sri. Aurobindo, Similarly in Poojya Appaji Dasoha has spread widely in all the aspects of life in an institutional form and developed into Mahadasoha.

Dr. S.A. Palekar
Prof. & Chairman
Dept. of Studies and Research in Political Science
Gulbarga University, Gulbarga.
Karnataka State, India

CONTENTS

PREFACE

There is a marvelous power in this universe. It is all-pervading, and is hidden in all animate and inanimate things in the universe. Just as there is self in body, in this universe also which is full of living beings, there are innumerable Selves which are part and parcel of the Supreme God. Each Self is a dwelling place of the Supreme God. So it is said: "Linga embodies the world". In other words, Linga contains the world and the world contains Linga.

Man is by nature inquisitive. He ever longs to know the eternal truth. This quest conducted in the outer world becomes science; but the same quest conducted within one's own Self leads to Self realization, and its pursuit becomes spiritual quest. Just as God is within ourselves, we are in God. God pervades the whole universe. Even then Self-realization, and through that God-realization, is not to be attained easily, and by each and everyone. Because between the Self and the Supreme Self there is the iron curtain of ego. It is not just the sheath of sugarcane as Basaveshwara describes it, it is a big thorn in the flesh of all the three worlds. All religions, religious founders, preceptors, sages, prophets and sharanas have tried to peel off the sugarcane sheath and to take out the thorn in the flesh, and have been doing it. The Vedas are supposed to be the key to the secret of destroying ego. So also the Upanisads, Vachanas and Mahadasoha Sutras. Like wise, the Holy Bible, the Holy Quran and other scriptures in the world are regarded as the master key to demolish the wall of ego. When the thick layer of ego in the form of pride and demolish the wall of ego. When the thick layer of ego in the form of pride and insolence covering the Self is removed, the Self shines with its original splendour, and no doubt, the Self becomes the Supreme Self.

The process of annihilation of ego should take place in all walks of life, that is, in eating, in dressing, in giving, in receiving etc., Let us take a common act of exchanging greeting. Greeting is not just a formality. There is love, reverence, devotion and God-realization in greeting one another. Hence greeting becomes on act of dasoha. Likewise, eating. If a person lives only to eat, what he eats becomes some stuff to fill his belly. If a person eats just to live, what he eats becomes food. It a person eats in order to live with the purpose of realizing God, what he eats becomes Prasada i.e., sacrament. Thus all actions and reactions in one's life become dasoha.

Dasoha does not refer only to outward act. It is a perennial process going on within and without a person. It is made clear in the *Mahadasoha Sutras* that the body-devotee is ever engaged in serving the life-breath Jangama. Whatever we enjoy through the five-fold sense organ–joys, tranquility of mind, peace etc., the inner Self also enjoys, and becomes a Self–witness to all that he does. It is said, "God is both the giver of food and the receiver (the one who eats it) of food". In this sense, everything done for the sake of Lord Shiva becomes Dasoha.

Man's greed is one of his weaknesses. "I want everything. Everything is mine."– this greediness is the root cause of sorrow. For examples, suppose a person is distributing sweets among children. Some boys desiring to get more, view with one another and dash at the person distributing sweets. With the result that the basket of sweets falls to the ground and all the sweets go waste. What do the greedy boys get in the end? Nothing; only distress. Thus, man's greed for everything leads him to disappointment and distress only. God has given us enough to meet our needs. He gives us all that is required for our living without asking. Before a child is born, the mother's breasts are stored with milk. We should go working without ego and giving without ego. Then we learn to treat both joys and sorrow with equanimity.

God is immortal, eternal and blissful. This world, created out of Him, longs to head straight for its original home, that is, heaven and to achieve immortality. Each creature tries to achieve immortality through its offspring, that is, through procreation. Man achieves immortality through marriage in the sense that he begets children through the marriage bond. Therefore, in the case of human beings marriage becomes a sacred bond, and *dosoha dharma.* Just as outwardly he enjoys the company of his spouse, inwardly too he enjoys the company of his spouse. In every man there are two selves–one male and the other female, and in every woman too there are two selves–male and female. The installation of the male and the female principles at each place of chakra in the human body speaks of the inseparable state of male and female principles in all creatures. That is why, Lord Shiva who is the source of the universe, is called Ardhanarishwara, meaning half-man and half-woman. The couple practicing dasoha physically beget the children who will continue the tradition of dasoha, and spiritually they attain liberation, that is, they meet the 'lady called Nirvana' hand in hand. On the physical plane, the bond between man and women becomes love, and the same bond on the spiritual plane becomes devotion. This devotion, with the help of Panchachara and Shatsthala, procures liberation for the daoshi couple. If devotion becomes Shiva's foot, liberation becomes. His crown, whether God is worshipped in the state with a from or without a form, unswerving devotion go God is sure to please Him and produce the desired result of liberation. At this juncture, I am reminded of an incident that took place while I was traveling by train towards Delhi. An Arabbi Professor was a co-passenger. On seeing the Istalinga round my neck, he asked me; "What is that thing?" I said, "It is the Istalinga which I worship thrice a day". Then he said, "God is formless. Do you call a stone piece God?" Then I asked him, 'While offering prayer to God you say Allah aloud. Is that word God?" To my question his answer was : "The word 'Allah' is a symbol of the formless God which prompts us and reminds us of God". Then I said gently and patiently, 'If to the eyes the stone piece is God, to the ears the sound of the word 'Allah' invokes God. Then how could your Allah be formless?" To the eyes God is visual and to the ears God is audible. Both the stone Linga and the world Allah are not God but symbols of God and have the attributes of God, one appeals to the eyes and the other to the ears. Just the utterance of Allah world brings to your mind the thought of God, the sight of the Linga on our palm brings to our eyes the thought of God. Our goal is the same God-realization. Only our ways are different." Then the Professor of Arabbi was fully convinced and pleased with my explanation.

In some religions charity is allowed only to the needy, but a *dasohi* does not discriminate between the rich and the poor. He sees divinity in all, and serves all with the same sense of humility. He sees God in beasts, birds and insects too and serves food to all and is pleased, when they are served and fed well.

One the whole, Mahadasoha Sutras unveil the spirit of dasoha hidden in the universe. Dasoha Dharma is universal, eternal and all-pervading. These Sutras are not deliberate creations, nor laboured productions. I just 'scribbled' them as and when they flashed into my mind at the behest of Lord Sharnbasveshwara. These principles are essential to redeem mankind. People should practice them and reap the blessings of Lord Sharnabasaveshwara who is both the giver and the receiver of gifts since he dwells in all of us. May Lord Sharnbasveshwara bestow peace and prosperity on all, and may the spirit of dasoha prevail in all!

Maha Dasoha Sutras composed by me in Kannada were earlier translated in English by Dr. Judith Kroll an American scholar and Prof. in English literature and Dr. L. Basavaraju Prof. from University of Mysore, Mysore, and 'Basava Purskar' a national awardee. Sri. M.V. Kamath, a noted journalist and presently Chairman of Prasara Bharati, Government of India, visited Lord Sharnbasveshwara Mahadashoa Peetha to get *darshan* and blessings of Lord Sharnbasveshwara. Inspired by the Maha Dasoha Sutras composed by me again he translated them in English and has given commentary on all 21 sutras in English language so that the English speaking people all over the world will be greatly benefited by a such a spiritual message & philosophy enshrined in the form of sutras in this book. May God bless Sri. M.V. Kamath. Serials Publications, New Delhi, also considered to publish this book as a matter of great honour and pious service to God. May God bestow peace and prosperity on all, and may the spirit of dasoha prevail in all.

His Holiness Dr. Sharnbasvappa Appa
Mahadasoha Peethadhipathi
Shri Sharnbasveshwar Samsthan, Gulbarga
Karnataka State – India

PART - I

INTRODUCTION

by

Poojya Dr. Sharnbasvappa Appa.

INTRODUCTION

Poojya Dr. Sharnbasvappa Appa

This great world is indeed a manifestation of magnificent and mysterious power. Before this profound and mysterious power, the power possessed by every object, organism in this world appears to be very tiny and insignificant. However, this power is a miniature form of that magnificent and mysterious power. Though that magnificent power is well within us but it appears not to our naked eyes and remains invisible and secret. As the soul is present within us similarly it is also present and pervading across the whole world. That imiminent magnificence in the world itself is God. That is why the Upanishads say God is omnipresent and omnipotent. They declared "Linga Maddhe Jagath Sarvam". It means the Linga is the manifestation of this world and the entire cosmos is well within Linga.

This can be better understood with an illustration. When you look at the high voltage electric power generated at a far off (distant) place, this power can be taken to any other place, no matter how far is the distance. But the power of its impact is so intact vigourous and strong. that it remains in the same high voltagic condition even when it is taken to a remote place. Its power is felt here as strong as it was at its original source. This power generated in a remote place is so powerful with its high voltage current that mammath and large-scale industries can be run with a help of this power, a remote dark place can be illuminated instantly with this electricity. Similarly God who is like this current is present everywhere. His spirit pervades everywhere. He is present in this nature, in all of us and all objects and organisms living or nonliving. But what does one need to realize him? For that one should cast off the pride and ego present in him or her once this is done as God is already present in him or her will be revealed like power in an electric bulb being illuminated when the button is switched on, unless and until the button is switched on the bulb will not be lit. Once the button is on the bulb will be lit. So here as the button acts as a dividing line acting as a strong barrier does not allow the bulb to contact with the current present in the wire. Similarly the tinge of egoism present in us will not allow to realize the God. Here the ego acts as a button. So to realize God by casting off ego as you illuminate the bulb by switching it on.

By nature, human beings are gifted with the faculty of thinking and ratiocination *i.e.* "jignas" or inquisitive nature, that is why human beings are not only far superior to animals but are also quite different from them and are unique, this is possible exclusively due to their faculty of thinking. The ever-busy man has been making ceaseless efforts everyday to discover the new truths so far hidden and covered and thus derives the supreme happiness and contentment from it. When man made efforts with his intelligence to discover and investigate the external powers (Bahari shakti) infinite compass (area), that it has been termed as science or it can also be termed as discovery. When the inquisition and meditation are used for discovering the internal truths, then it becomes spiritualism. With their own spiritual experiences the proclamation of the realized souls, like the great seers, saints, visionaries and mystics, is that, the colossal, invisible latent power and energy is secretly manifested within us and thus it is said that "Yatra Jeevah Tatra Shivah" that means where there is life there is

God. As God is present within us with all His infinite immense power, in the same way we too are present within him. Similarly the whole universe is manifested in God. If this is the case we get a series of questions like, where is the God of such an immense and infinite power? How does He look like? What is His form? What should we do to visualize and realize him? Or what is to be done to have his glimpses? With their profound inquisition, the great souls, who has the wealth of realization and rich spiritual experience, made an introspection and declared thus-though the soul is an alter ego of God, yet there is a sheath of egoism, which separates each other and does not allow to understand each other. The main task or act of spiritualism is to remove this sheath or layer of ignorance (or dispel the darkness) by making discovery of the internal world, as is done in the discovery of the external world.

It is very important to realize " Paramatma" through "Atma, so it is a pilgrimage of the soul from self to, beyond the contours of self, it's a journey from already known to unknown. It is very important and quite essential to know that, we must realize the God through our self or soul only. So it is imperative that going beyond self is through self-only. Since Jeeva-th life, Jagattu-the world, paramatma-the God or soul are so beautifully fused and well inter-woven into each other that, they can not be distinguished as each is made up of the other and the spirit of each pervades into the other. This reminds us the trinity concept. It is indeed a revelation to learn that, here is a religion which one can deem without any wavering and follow that, it is practicing religion. Here every one is privileged to seep Paramatama through his own Atma that is seeking and realizing God through his own self. It is indeed a divine process of going beyond self through self only.

So when the spiritual activities are extended beyond the inward deeds to the deeds taking place even outwardly also, they too become the deeds of spiritualism. Similarly when we offer the same to the other persons, it is nothing but an extension of the spiritual deeds. Then who is offering all these here? It is almighty God Himself. So God is the greatest Dasohi. But this puts forth a prerequisite condition that, we should shun away the long nurtured and deeply rooted egoism.

All the religions in the world, the religious teachers, the saints, seers, crusaders and sharanas have all tried and made efforts ceaselessly to shun away this sheath of egoism, call it by any name like religion, mysticism, etc. Initially those who rooted out this sheath of egoism have emerged as spiritual leaders and prophets and established their religions. The seers, sages, and the spiritual leaders were all blessed with golden keys to shun away this bark of illusion. Thus we have today the same keys, which have become the Vachanas, Sutras, Kuran, Bible and all the scriptures. As an opthalmologist removes the thin layer or cataract developed in the eyes by means of surgery and helps to regain the real vision. Similarly, we too are deeply affected by the layer of ego, Artha, Prana, Abhiman. If this layer is removed, the God within us will be revealed, who is the replica of our own or self-image and Swanubhava.

> When the honeycomb is built upon a sugar cane,
> They do not relish the sweetness of each other,
> A sheath called Arth, prana, Abhimana,
> Acts as a barrier between Bhakta and jangama,
>
> *—So sings Kudala Sangama deva.*

From time immemorial man has pursued different religions across the world. Though man has trodden different paths or religions to seek God, yet all these paths and religions have taken him to one destination, that destination is the Destination of God. Seeking God is like tasting the sweetness of sugar-cane, in different forms, some may prefer to relish it by a romantic style of biting it with their teeth directly and some may relish sugar-cane by cutting it into different pieces and Yet some other may go for crushing it, extracting its juice and then relish it by drinking. This analogy makes it amply clear that though the means are different to seek the God yet their objective of realization of God is the same. So experiencing God is like relishing the sweetness of sugar cane finally by adopting different means and methods. But this needs the shunning away of egoism or pride, which is the source of all diseases.

As the honey comb is built upon the sugar cane neither of them can taste the sweetness of each other; in the same way, due to the presence of sheath called Artha (money), Prana (life), and abhiman (pride or egoism) between Bhakta, the devotee and jangama, the God act as an obstacle. Here we can further observe that God who is the milk of human kindness and benevolence is sheathless, walless and filled with sweetness like a honey comb, so here the honey comb is sheathless. So also the God, whereas the sugar cane is shealthful, so also the man, a barrier that forbids man, the divine company of God, as the sugar cane is deprived of the Sweet company of honeycomb. So here the honeycomb is sheathless. Here the honeycomb represents the God and the Sugar cane represents the man.

It is magnificent to see that Basaveshwara has recognized in this vachana, the relationship between the devotee and God (Bhakta and Jangama) through a finest pleasing simile. As epic writers arrest and depict majestic beauty in their works through similes. This enthralling spiritual simile divulges Shiva-darshan through Atmadarshana or the divine vision of the soul i.e. the realization of God through self-alone. This simile standing as an eternal teacher and preacher disseminates and reveals forever the pathway to God, acting as a forefinger depicting the Truth, God and Beauty.

Even when the honeycomb is built upon the sugar cane, neither of them relishes the sweetness of the other, owing to the stumbling block in the form of a bark or a sheath. Similarly Artha (money) Prana (life) Abhimana (pride or egoism) which exist in every human being like a bark and prevent him from realizing the God, who is present well within himself. But God is devoid of that bark. God, is like a complete and perfect honeycomb. There is no vaccum in God. He is complete, he is omnipotent and omnipresent. All the saints, seers, scriptures, religions and their principles aim at shedding down or removing this sheath. The paramount and fundamental principal of Dasoha is to cast off this egoism. Nirahankar is what the Dasoha dharma aims at and perceives. The lifeline of Dasoha philosophy is Nirahankar. Only when we cast off this sheath of ahankara or egoism that indeed opens hitherto closed gates of truth, God and beauty. Then only we can have the glimpses of these, which are the epitomes of our own self. Then what a celebration of life, becoming blessed one i.e. divine and ultimately becoming Godly. Then God himself epitomizes in the form of supreme bliss and ecstasy (that is Sacchidanda swaroopa). Shivayogi Siddharameshwar gives us a finest and most beautiful precept to castoff egoism.

All the people of the three worlds have been greatly affected with the pricking of one thorn. If man could be pricked with one thorn he would certainly suffer till it is removed, otherwise he would be restless, similarly, if all the people of the world are pricked by a single thorn, then imagine, which is that thorn? That lethal thorn is, the thorn of pride and egoism. If man wants to be calm and quiet and lead a tranquil life and have a peaceful disposition and bliss, he certainly needs to root out the deadly and lethal thorn called pride. Indeed the religion plays a vital role and functions effectively in uprooting this thorn of pride. Hence it becomes obligatory on our part to think and meditate upon this issue and seek the pathway to eternal peace in all earnest.

When God descended down to earth
Became Linga by being static,
Janagama by moving
Guru by realizing

—So proclaimed the sharanaas.

This is indeed a beautiful concept of God, as finest gift by sharanaas to our fellow human beings. Even Upanishath pronounces' Ishaa Vaasham Idam Jagath. Sarwam' *i.e.*—God is omnipresent, the world is a manifestation of the almighty God, his spirit pervades everywhere. That is why—

Salutations and obeisance to Guru
Salutations and obeisance to Linga
Salutations and obeisance to Jangama

Salutations and respects must be offered to God who is in different forms Like Guru, Linga, Jangama, enlightenment, finest knowledge, wisdom, great scholars, towering personalities, noble objectives and values, these are all the manifestations and transfiguration of God himself. Love blooms and blossoms where there is a self-surrender, pride or ego melts away where there is a love. A devotional salutation performed in person with reverence becomes Dasoha. This the highest and finest kind of Dasoha, which is nothing but worshipping, paying salutations or respects should not result in a mere dry act of formality. It should transcend the boundaries of formality. So salutation should be performed, having intense and profound faith realising that God dwells in that they act itself. If we salute the realised souls with love, our souls too get enlightenment and awareness. Even respecting and greeting mutually creates good-will and thus it results into shivadarashana. (Divine Company of God) and Dasoha prapti (The granting of abounding Dasoha), Dasoha is nothing but salutation and service to God, Dasoha is nothing but worshipping. Indeed love begets from there, that is why the term 'Sharanu' or salutation has become a 'sutra' (formula) and in turn, it has become a key to successful living and spiritualism.

When we go to a holy places like church, temple or mosque and meet someone at the premises of such a holy place, we salute him, realizing that there is God well within him. We salute him with abiding love and with deep devotion; because there is god, there is soul, in himself as well. So there will be realization of soul present in both of them, the one who salutes and the one who receives it.

If lived for eating, it
Becomes stuff
It eaten for living, it
Becomes food
If eaten for spiritualism it
Becomes sacrament.

It is a human tendency to segregate and keep away the body from the soul when we offer food to body, the soul within us, is a witness to it. Because where there is life, there is soul. So we feed the soul with food, for the sustenance of life and the soul witnesses it. The body walks for this soul, the body serves the soul, the soul sees through the eyes, the soul hears through the ears. If life lives, the soul witnesses. Through all senses the body serves this soul. So when any individual seeks pleasure and enjoys through his five senses, they are being experienced by god himself, and he himself is witness to it. Akkamahadevi a great celestial soul had humbly dedicated her body and soul to God without having even least attachment either over her bodily pleasures or the pleasures of soul as she attributed them to the God almighty, Akkamahadevi got awareness through her soul, her soul was connected and related to higher soul and inner soul. Therefore God experienced her body. She considered God as her celestial husband and her body as the source of God's pleasure. So God could derive a highest pleasure from her body. Nothing belonged to her neither the body nor the pleasure of the body as both the body and the pleasure were dedicated to God.

This is how she nobalised and divinised by bringing in, the devine touch of God to the body and its pleasures which ordinary people think of as base and frivolous activity. For

Akkamahadevi the blossoming of her soul was a smile. So God witnesses, when the food is offered and the soul relishes it. Similarly the body too relishes it and God witnesses it. Offering food with a realization that there is a soul deep within us; it becomes sacrament, that is why there is service (Dasoha) even among the nine doors of the body (navalingsakeegalu). No religion is greater than service. Service to humanity is service to God, this is indeed very individualistic and humanistic and we should offer every marshel of food we consume for God, and then it becomes sacrament instead of food.

There is a relentless act of Dasoha being performed ceaselessly deep within each one of us, where everyone's Kaya (body) is Bhakta (devotee) and prana (life) is Jangama (God). This service-taking place inwardly is complimentary to the service-taking place outwardly. This service rendered externally influences and encourages, the internal or inward service. If we offer delicious food with full of aroma to the soul (God) present within us through our sense organ-nose, with unwavering sacrosanct feeling and realizing with soul as its witness that there is soul within us, then it becomes sacrament.

If we offer sumptuous and delicious food to our soul through our tongue with the soul as witness, then it becomes a sacrament. If we offer visible lush green or any scenic beauties to our soul through our eyes with the soul as a witness, then it becomes sacrament (Prasad).

If we offer beautiful melodies or hymns in the praise of God to our soul, through our ears with the soul as witness, then it becomes Prasad. If we offer a pure and pristine touch to our soul through our skin with the soul as witness, then it becomes sacrament. If we offer pleasure, bliss or joy to our soul through our mind, with the soul as a witness, then it becomes sacrament or prasad.

The sacrosanct and altruistic service rendered to our soul, which is present deep within us, through the body, mind feelings and emotions is being witnessed by our soul or self, then it becomes sacrament or prasad.

All our pleasures, happiness, tranquility, wealth and peace sought through our five sense organs are accepted by god present in us as a witness. "Dhata bhogatha Swayam Shivha". *i.e.* God alone is the cause who grants every thing and accepts every thing; realizing the essence of this thought, if done every thing in the name of God and attributing it to him, then it becomes service (Dasoha). Then this physical body with all its flesh and blood gets converted or transcended into Mantra Pinda' or heavenly body or merges into the cosmic soul. There is such an enticement in God that there is celestial beauty. The divine company of God is almost like the affectionate and ever caring lovely company of a beloved. The company of God is— as sweet as, electrifying as the company of the ladylove. Akka Mahadevi in fact hankered for the divine company of the God, where in she found both her lover and the God in him. She found and sought her husband in the God himself and in the divine grace of the God. Although one is in flesh and blood like Akka mahadevi one should transmute all the bodily activities, eternal love, devotion and everything that is physical and spiritual into divine acts of God.

Every holy place is either resided by God or the divine souls who have gone there and resided. Either the place where they have gone and resided is being divinised and spiritualized by the divine souls or the place, which is divine innately, has enticed the spiritual souls to reside there. Hence the human beings keep flocking to such a holy place or abode forever. Working for the sake of livelihood is just an ordinary life. Working for the sake of livelihood but also for the welfare of others is a good cultured life. Working not only for the sake of livelihood but also for the welfare of others thinking that serve to humanity is service to God is Kayaka-Dasoha.

Unmindful of the existence of our fellow human beings, if we work and live by ourselves, enjoying the fruits of our labour, it becomes just an ordinary life. To this category all the animals, birds and all the living organisms belong. They too perform their act, work for themselves and live by themselves just like human beings. So this kind of living is a mere existence but not a living. Because there is no distinction between man and other creatures as the objectives of both and the function they perform are the same. If man eats for life then he too belongs to classification of animals, because he is a social animal. The high point of any culture is or lies in serving self as well as serving all that is an altruistic service. When man becomes a focal point of happiness and bliss, he makes others also to fall in his influence. When such people work and reap the fruits of their labour, they just do not confine it to their life alone. There is easy access for one and all to share their fruits as well as their happiness and bliss. Such people are indeed, better than those, who live by themselves. The lives of the people of this category indeed depicts a good cultured life. It is a welcome sign of man's better living and progress. It is said that, when this kind of life lived earlier, the culture among human being rather sprouted from there. When people started cultivating land with mutual Cooperation, further the culture started, when agriculture started. At this stage human beings are better placed, as they have been able to shout down their natural savagery instinct, without being harmful. They have great concern for their fellow human beings. "joy for self and enjoy with all" becomes their lifeline and life quintessence.

Above all these, there is another kind of living, a higher living, a divine living, that living is called Kayaka Dasoha, sublime and sacrosanctal, cultured life. At this stage man not only works and enjoys the fruit of his labour but at the same time, he makes other also happy and shares the fruit of his labour with them. This kind of activity gives him a profound happiness and bliss. Further he goes ahead and dedicates all this to God. He realizes the very presence of God in all such activities undertaken by him. Life indeed becomes a celebration as man extends his joy and happiness to others and feels and realizes they very presence of God.

This is the difference between ordinary life, cultured life and Kayaka-Dasoha, sublime and sacrosanct culture. It is inevitable for people living in the whole world that they have to carry on and practice, some times knowingly some times unknowingly the important triple deeds or acts, like performing, offering and receiving, the acts of performing, offering and receiving or accepting become deeds of service (acts of dasoha) only when all these deeds are free from the sheath of pride or ego. Then our life becomes meaningful and our existence a living. The altruistic service (Dasoha Jeeva) is possibly only when the welfare and the goodwill of all the living beings are wished and taken care of. Such deeds of Dasoha or service should be practiced in every way of life. When our life and character are moulded in the anvil ego, then there is no scope for a better living. So we should cast off egoism, so that our mere existence becomes meaningful and our existence becomes a grand living, as we all know, man being finite is being directly controlled by the spell of egoism. Ego supports and follow man wherever he goes. As the ego grows richer and richer, we are made to look smaller and smaller, poorer and poorer. But when we attain infinity, then the ego nurtured within us melts away naturally and automatically. Ego extincts, where Linga (God) exists. So the grand way and the royal path to cast off this deadly and lethal ego is to surrender to God. So man needs the divine company of the great souls and divine people (sathsanga). Then the life, which is swayed and encircled by ego, is set free and man never indulges in petty things, as man himself is a part of infinity. Hence his existence is already there in infinity. So his attainment of infinity from finiteness enables him to occupy this world without being occupied, then he will have a detached attachment to this world. So surrendering to God makes him a divine darling of God. Because the magnificence of infinity crumbles the finiteness.

So always indulge in serving without nurturing ego. God loves such people and such people endear God. What a synchronization of relations between God and man.!

That is why

A Dasohi is one who knows nothing but offering,
A Dasohi is one who teaches nothing but offering,
A Dasohi is one who practices nothing but offering,
And that Aroodha Dasoha is Dasohi of highest order.

When the spirit of Dasoha (service) becomes a part and partial of our life or when it is transmitted into our lives, it aims at the welfare of each and every living being. Man should be magnanimous and generous enough to offer. Even he should not be poor in imagining and giving also. Even literature written, to serve the purpose of dasoha also is a kind of service. But when this literature and its spirit is practices, it becomes culture, serving is possible even in ordinary life also, the cannons or principles of Dasoha or dasohasiddhi lie in assimilating and influencing and transmuting it in every walk and act of our life.

If good deeds are to be practiced and adhered to in our day-to-day life, the legacy of our culture and tradition influences very much and plays a very important role. It is like leading our lives in the light of illustrious great souls who held the torches and guided us eternally. The divine company of great people and divine souls is a must for the elevation of our own lives and it is indeed possible, when we seek God with all humility it is true that we all need a sort of God-intoxication. We should repose a grand faith in God and keep modesty, have upright character, noble virtues that indeed launch us from this finiteness to infinity that is abode of God. So the highest form of Dasoha (service) or good Culture is rooted in serving others selflessly. Dasoha which aims at the Serving of others, also expects from us a good culture and tradition.

It becomes Kayaka
When egotism is disfigured
And performance is devoid of I feeling
It becomes Dasoha when egotism is aberrated
And offering is devoid of I feeling
Receiving without I feeling.
With sacrosanctal devotion becomes sacrament.

Therefore either man should live in infinity or live with God. God does not reside apart from us, God is present in all of us. But we are ignorant of his presence in us due to ego. But great souls have realization of God, which, they could attain by shedding down ego. God is present in the great teacher, spiritual leaders and realized souls (Ballantha Mahantas). But we human beings must derelict and extinct this egotism from us; so that, we can long for godhead from the stage of an ordinary mortal being. It certainly becomes easier to get his grace and merge with God and seek his divine company for those who have inherited a spiritual legacy as in case of lineages of Sharanabasaveshwar Where in the spiritual empire has already been built. There is a rich legacy of culture and tradition from time immemorial.

So,

The divine act or work
Done, ego-less or without the involvement of pride
Becomes performance
It is not an ordinary performance
When done ego less, it is a divine performance.
It is not an ordinary offering
When done casting off egotism, it becomes a divine offering.
It is not an ordinary receiving.
When done shunning away ego, it become divine receiving.

The cannons and principles of Kayaka, Dasoha and Prasada are deeply embedded and rooted in every acts of doing-driving away the pride, offering casting off the self, and receiving derelecting and extincting the ego. These are the three cardinal truths of God or Shiva-Sutragalu like the Arya Sutragalu or Mahatma Buddha.

Doing with devotion, offering with devotion, receiving with devotion are all the acts of Sahaja prasada or natural sacraments. But man's greed for excessive possession, lays him in bottomless deep sorrows. Look at the birds and their activities. They never complain of shortage of food or anything. But human beings restlessly keep craving for more and more. But the God, the creator is benevolent enough to store enough milk in the breasts of mother in advance, even before the child is born. A just born infant or child need not struggle for its food or sustenance. An apt instance can be cited here to illustrate this thought. Let us assume, a person is distributing sweets to a gathering of boys from his basket, some boys who have no patience enough due to their greed, want more and more sweets, in the process, they would get collide with him and eventually, they might even fall on him which would result into the fall of all sweets from the container. Owing to this none of them would get sweets and those who do not succeed in getting sweets are obviously unhappy and sorrowful.

Bhagavathgeeta proclaims "Karmannewadhikaraste, Malphalesu Kadaachana", Mahatma Buddha has declared that the excessive greed is the root cause of all sorrows. Basava and other Sharanas heralded that, God grants bounty if you do it without any least expectation of anything and without the feeling of the involvement of the sense. Dasoha Sutras say God grants abundantly every thing that is sought if you do or serve without the feeling that you have done it. "Maadidenembudu Manadali Holedare, Barisitu Shivana dangura" that is, if a feeling creeps into your mind that you are the cause and instrumental for that performance, then, God will awaken you by bringing you to conscience, by beating the drum of awareness. On several occasions the long nurtured desires of man are not fulfilled. Sometimes one gets all his wishes granted providentially and naturally, even without least expectations. This can happen and is possible only when we distill our feelings from the infection of pride or ego, that is why:

If you perform doing away with
The involvement of the self
God grants you, even when you
Do not ask for.

One gets the bliss when one performs shunning away the pride with a dutiful mind and in turn it becomes a Shivasamkriti or supreme culture, even one might attain equanimity or composure of mind.

God the supreme being and the creator of this universe is immortal and also a paragon of eternal bliss (Nitya Anandamayi). This universe which is an offspring of God is heading towards eternity there is a Divine design in nature that is, the longing for eternity. Every living being or organism, be it a plant, bird, animal or man, living in this nature attain immortality relentlessly through the unique process of procreations which is indeed the will of the God, and also his own creation. Man is also supposed to be deathless (Amrut putra) as he has been immortalized from one generation to the other through the process of procreation. Man being the finest and glorious manifestation of God and inalienable part and partial of him with the objective of immortality, lives in perfect bliss and experiences the ecstasy of God. The society where man lives has developed the institution of marriage to achieve a holy, pristine and harmonious relationship and have an innate culture of absolute bliss.

Marriage is sweet, sweeter is the bond of relationship,
Beautiful and handsome is the mutual relationship of two bodies;
Happiness is what the mutual bonds of two minds get,
Supreme bliss is what the mutual bondage of the two souls seek.

It is an important imperative to be noticed that the sex is only a passion, with love it is only the physical activity, but the higher activity is that, where the composition starts from soul, then the passion ceases, there is not only soul to soul, physical, but also metaphysical and spiritual communion. Because God's soul is coaxing. It is indeed an act of divinity; base and frivolous thinking in this context is indeed sacrilegious.

When the distinction of man is towards eternity through the natural law of the world called procreation. The husband and wife are never the stumbling blocks to the world of spiritualism to attain Godhead or transcendentalism. In fact the family life is complimentary to the spiritualism and even inspires spiritualism. In married life there is nothing to hide; married people are more transparent. Life is serene, placid and unperturbed,

> Asthavaran is the Dwelling place of Sharana-Sati, Linga Pati, Vibhuti, Rudrakshi, Mantras are the decoratives or ornaments of Sharanasati,
> And the affectionate intense talks.

All these ornaments speak abundantly the love of God for a devotee and create and enrich an environment of divinity. In this worldly life the enchanting and lovely words spoken by the lady and her fragile heart with full of love, enthrall and win the mind of her husband. Even a devotee becomes worthy of God's liking and love, if he lives a life always in eternal love, unwavering devotion, impeccable dedication, altruism, practice of the Panchacharas and showing interest in Sacchinanda. In a serene spiritual atmosphere even the devotee attains the Godhead or shivaswaropa (self--actualization) realization of God through self. The omnipotent God and the soul who is present in all of us, is a witness to all the activities that take place within us. It is the God who experiences the sight we see, the sound we listen to, the touch we experience and the taste we relish. As we consider consuming food as Anna Brahma. So, we are eating and relishing through our food-God only, which in turn becomes prasad. These are called "Navalinga Sakeel" or nine doors of the body as God is present in all parts of the world. Though we search God and make efforts to see him in the world outside yet, he is present deep within ourselves. Though he is sought deep within our cord, yet he is present deep within souls in the form of our own self. When we bounce a ball on the ground or hit it against a wall, the ball rebounds. Here the ball itself is not rebounding on its own but the energy that we exert upon it causes the rebounding; similarly God too is present within us, we should seek him and realize him within ourselves like the energy in the above mentioned parable of which we are unaware of and misconstrued thinking that the ball is rebounding on its own, negating our own potentiality or energy. Most of us are not in a position to seek God as we are following only the shadow, seeking only skeleton but not wisdom and knowledge, we must just work because, good work itself is a reward. The fruit that we get is only a shadow, so we must keep seeking good work, because nobody can give us a good work. But they may give us an award for good work. That is why good work itself is a reward.

"What is the bond between the world here and hereafter?
As Sharana sati Linga pathi declared
The lovely bond with wife is love
The eternal love kept in God transcends into devotion and becomes Bhakti Dasoha".

The above lines of Mahadasoha Sutra amply explicit and focus on the relationship between life here and life hereafter, the worldly life and spiritual life, against the tantric background. The Shivasharanas in this way recognized the Shat-chakras in the body of a person in yogic terminology.

There are six chakras in the body of a male, they are— Mooladhara, Swadistana, Manipooraka, Anahata, Vishuddhi, Agna, Guda, Guhya, Naabhi, Hrudaya, Kaand, Bhrunaadhy are the places of Shat-chakraas respectively. It has been considered that there is a purusha and a Shakti respectively for every two units of chakra. That is why every man is a composition of purusha shakti. That is why shiva is called Ardhanaarishwara. At Conceptual level, woman is not a woman and man is not a man. Half woman is present in man already and half man is present in woman already.

That is why a person may like only few women whom he likes. This reflects that here, his own shadow is mirrored in her, he finds himself in her. So every organism present in the nature is a blend or synthesis purusha-shakti. Through the progeny of this union, immortality is attained. If external enternity attained that development attains inmortality (Amrutatva-immortal blis) internally. This world, which we trod on, acts as a spiritual ladder for climbing the world here after. But definetly it never acts as on abstacle or hurdle. Internally at the first stage of everyone. Moolodhara is purusha and swadhistana is Shakti. At the second stage manipooraka becomes purusha.

Anaahata becomes Shakti. At the third stage vishuddi becomes purusha and Agnya becomes shakti.

Contrary to this among women, at first stage Mooladadhara is Shakti and Swadhistana is purusha. At the second stage Manipooraka becomes Shakti and Anahat becomes purusha. At the third stage Vishuddhi becomes Shakti and Agnya becomes Purusha.

In this way internally every man and woman posses innately the purusha (male) and Shakti (female), Chakra, as it is present in the nature. The Shat-chakras play an important and vital role in developing and fostering the feeling of love and feeling of harmony or synchronization among the men and women. When the feminine chakraa or cycle gets awakened in man, he desires and longs a woman. Who has such shades out side. When the purushachakra gets awakened in women, she longs or desires a man who has such shades outwardly. Even Veerashaivaas mention about these chakraas which the Tantriks speak of. Even they have adapted them in Shutsthalas.

When man and woman get attracted mutually in the material world, they come together and create shakti or power in the form of a child. When this progeny is continued ceaselessly it takes them to immortality. Similarly a Saadhaka rises step by step and attains self-realization with the help of the power of his devotion, which is destined deep within himself. Then devotion becomes the feet of Parashiva and salvation or Mukti becomes his Mukuta or head.

In worldly life, the feeling of love becomes instrumental for reaping the fruit. But in the world of spiritualism, the same feeling of love becoming eternal transcends into Bhaktibhava eternal (eternal deep-devotion) and in turn becomes instrumental to attain salvation. Love begets love. Devotion also begets love.

A sadhaka through the Shatchakraas present deep within himself will rise stage by stage and this has been recognized or found by the Veerashivas in Shatsthalas.

When Mooladadhara called Purusha and Swadhistan called shakti get confluenced, deep within Sadhaka, the shakti or energy starts flowing, Bhakti Bhaava (deep and eternal devotion) starts growing. Here love transcends into faith and faith transcends into love, mutually, eternal love transcends into shruddhe or devotion and finally culminates into the stage of Bhakta or devotee. When that devotion gets dedicated and with full faith free from doubts then, he becomes Mahesh (God). This act which occurs (on its own) naturally without any inspiration of any sort is called Yogakriya or an act of yoga. So faith in God is faith in love and vice-versa.

The power that is generated at the first stage rises in upward direction. Then Manipooraka called Purusha and Anahata called shakti present on it get fused and produce new power and that starts flowing downward, that creation is nothing but a state of Avadhaana, Bhakti, bhaava, prasaad and Anubhaava Bhaktibhaava called Pranalignga.

The infinite power generated deep within us raises in upward direction and at the third stage the vishuddhi called purusha, Agny called shakti get fused and the result is the shakti starts flowing and it also becomes the cause for the creation of Mahashakti. The forms of that Mahasakti are happiness, bliss and devotion, this stage is called the Sharanasthala, the feeling of harmonious Aikyasthala, the stage of fusion or harmony. Here union of purusha shakti takes place due to Avinabhava relation. From that power even god cannot be separated. That is why Sharanas have proclaimed that Sharanasati (the wife). Lingapati (the husband). The finest among purusha shakti chakras present deep within us are at the third stage chakras. Here sharanasati lingapati becoming one or merging into each other then attain the stage of Swayambhu (self-actualization) and Sacchidanada or bliss and reap infinite happiness and bliss and finally attain self revelation by being completely free and independent or liberated. This stage is called sunyasthiti, Aiyakyasthiti i.e. self actualization by the veerashaivas. Buddha christened it Nirvana and Jains termed it Moksha. However, the spiritual leaders of world religions have given different terminologies to this.

When worldly love gets eternalised it attains the Bhakti-Swaroopa the stage of devotion. That is why the impeccable and immaculate love becomes a meditation. If the love in the external world gives Rathi Sukha (devine bliss). The eternal love of the internal world getting deepened and concentrated gives Aatma rati sukha.

When Akkamahadevi was able to derive the divine pleasure of her soul's craving, she mentions in her vachana in a candid way so naturally. She says "Linga experiences the pleasure of my body". As she had experienced the God's intoxication and realized shiva. Hence, she attributed the pleasure of her body to God only and felt enlightened the shivaswarup within herself.

The wife in this wordly life plays a divine role and is a spiritual ladder to climb the spiritual world. That is why Sharanas have aptly said "Sativididu Nirvana Sati Kaanu" that is, realize the Nirvana sati (spiritual wife) through ones own wife alone. In this worldly life, wife is not an obstacle to the divine life. She is in fact instrumental in the divine life.

When our love in wife gets immortalized, it becomes devotion and dedication internally and flows in the form of Shakti. Sacchidanada Swaroopa (attaining the transcendental stage) is nothing but realization of Brahmananda; Shivananda and Linganada Swaroopa through Atmaratisukha or seeking the divine pleasure of the soul.

If a (Sadhaka) spiritual practitioner wants to be worthy of God's love, he must inculcate some of the practices in his life. When a person is suffering from weakness, in order to improve his health, he takes nutritious food and makes regular exercises with great interest. Similarly, a devotee has to infuse in his life some of the practices (Saadhanas) in order to attain transcendentalism. Those five practices are the panchaachaaraas.

Truth is God, God is truth. Lingachara (Practice of Lingachara) Dasoha is nothing but meticulous practicing and adhering to truth and God externally and seeking revelation or self-actualization through the divine inspiration of internal spiritual experience.

It is a fact and natural habit or instinct or call it even a desire of every human being to possess lovely and beautiful objects or things of embellishment. Similarly Athma (soul) cannot exist or live independently apart from paramathma (God), that is called Lingachar knowing truth is different from experiencing and becoming truth. Truth is nothing but the realisation of soul. As Isthalinga symbolizes the realization of the soul for that we have to concentrate through symbol to soul so that it helps us in such a way that by concentrating on soul and hence it should not be separated. It should be worn on our body. Through soul only one has to think, eat, act and perform all other activities.

Sadachara is nothing but a ceaseless practicing of meditation and a soulful offering of prayer to the God, who is an embodiment of purity, truth and goodness; he is one who practices always truth, so he is a champion of truth.

The three inevitable acts or spheres of life like working or labouring, offering and receiving. These acts are suffused with divinity or the practices of Shiva, then it is called Shivachar. To be more precise, let me explain in simpler terms. Truth is Shiva or God. God is truth, God is eternal love, So live a life full of eternal love.

The first foot of God is love through which one can reach the pinnacle of God i.e. Mukuta, that is bliss, then you attain (become) bliss. Love for all creatures is a must. We can't live without God as God is love. So, live a godly life (i.e. truthful life); speak a Godly life (truthful life) practice a godly life (i.e. truthful life) since God is truth, and truth is God, when you speak of truth, you are speaking of god, so when you speak of truth that is nothing but Ananda or happiness. So, when you practice God *i.e.* Truth, in doing, giving and in receiving, then you get, and become sathchitananda-*i.e.* bliss. Because life is full of truth, love, shiva (God) and beauty. That is indeed divinity. So, eternal happiness is not away from us. It is in our deeds and practices because joy is forever, truth is forever, love is forever and beauty is forever when they are strictly practiced in our day today life.

So, working with devotion by casting off the feeling of pride and visualizing or realizing God in that very act is called kayaka. An egoless and pride less offering is Dasoha. Accepting with pure mind and devotion rooting out the feeling of self is Shivaprasad.

In this way, when every act of life is impregnated with the divine spirit of shiva (God) it becomes Shivachar (practicing god in all activities and deeds).

Uprooting the impediments and stumbling blocks that come in the path of spiritualism is Ganaachaar; it is here we see the highest culture of man, the culture at its best and the culture at, the full bloom and Zenith. This can be illustrated with a suitable instance, when a group of people are busy in conversation, suppose if one of them gets a mobile phone call if he is not able to talk on his phone and not able to stop others from talking, then he would certainly go out attend the call and return. The hidden inference of this instance is—Perform your task in such a way by which, neither your fellow beings are affected nor your personal work is hampered. This is called Ganaachar.

If a realized soul who is in form of Guru, Jangama, Sharana and even in form of a needy or poor person where we see souls in them is served with great devotion, dedication and grand humility, then that act is called Bhrithyachar.

Indian culture and philosophical thoughts are not only the most ancient one in the world but they do have a glorious legacy of tradition and are also highly revered and equally rich and popular. Although there are some lecunas, yet in all aspects the Indian religion and philosophy have prospered beyond the comprehension of human thought. These lecunas help the future generation to enable and take the religion to yet greater and greater heights and perfection. It is mainly due to our Indian religion and culture which have not been founded by one man because it has been enriched and sanctified by the extraordinary contribution of many thinkers, sages, seers, philosophers and saints. In this glorious tradition all the five senses of human beings have been cultured and noblelised. But it is equally important to learn that the five senses are not complete in themselves as they have been finite in nature with enough limitations. For instance the eye has its own limitations, it is not complete as it happens to be only an attribution, similarly the ear too has its own limitations, it is also incomplete it is also an attribution. But it is very relevant to learn that one can go to infinity from infiniteness. Nothing forbids anybody from attaining this infiniteness. Another important contribution of Indian culture and thinking is, along with this, the literature, music, art, fine art, dance like Bharatha-Natyam, Kuchipudi have not only been complimentary but are also supportive of spiritualism. The Indian philosophical thought has absorbed and conceived the spirit and essence of all these and is also a manifestation of them, that is why the Indian spiritual field is supposed to be a glorious tradition of excellent culture. All religions of the world have a deep dipping in Indian culture and they are mirrored here.

At this stage I am reminded of one of my early experiences. Once I was traveling in a train and my co-passenger happened to be a professor of Arabi of Delhi University. To my pleasant surprise, he instantaneously initiated and drove me into an interesting and absorbing discussion.

The question that he asked me was "May I know what are you wearing in your neck?" I answered with great interest "This is Istalinga, I worship it, I consider it as symbol of God". The very next question that he put one was "Isn't God formless, why do you call this stone, God, which has a form?" But in turn I asked him a question, though I knew asking him a question was not logical and pertinent, but yet I put a question to him, since the answer for his question was my question itself. I told him thus "When you pray you pronounce the word 'Allah!' then do you mean to say that the word Allah is God?". This was my question, for which he replied in this way. The word 'Allah' is formless. But God is not only formless but He is also nameless ("Naamaathita"). When we attribute God to that word, it makes us realize that there is God". To his explanation and reply, I explained with great patience in this way; when the sense organ 'eye' perceives 'Unga' carved in stone; similarly, the sense organ ear perceives idol in the word "Allah" then how is it that the word Allah is formless? When the object seen by the eyes cannot be heard by ears similarly, the words heard by ears cannot be seen by the sense organ eye. That is why the object, which becomes idol, the sense organ eyes, similarly, the word becomes idol to the sense organ ear, in the same way the smell becomes an idol to the sense organ nose. In this way the taste is an idol to the sense organ tongue. Touch is an idol to the sense organ skin. When this explanation was given, the Arabi professor made a revaluation of the notion that, he had held for his religion and pride he had nurtured for years and was dumb founded, realizing that all the religions teach the same principles and canons and started looking at all religions with a sense of equality, the foremost point to be remembered in this context is the base of formlessness is, form, the journey is always form to formlessness, from known to unknown, from man to God.

As god's image is attributed to the pronunciation of the word 'Allah' and as the God is reminded, when this word is uttered, similarly, through 'Istalinga' we realize the God and there is a system of seeing the self-image.

In this modern world, if we say, "We listen only to radio, but do not see television" is nothing short of our backwardness and also certainly not a sign of pride. It is indeed a sign of degradation and deterioration.

Among the five sense organs the most influential sense organ is eye. It is always good to take the use of the objects, which have greater influence, we undertake many activities and succeed in performing them in a better way by taking use of our sense organs, for instance listening to radio is one sided, reading literature is also one sided. If the same literature or the radio message is enacted on a stage or shown through a film, it is indeed more effective. To be more precise when we hear lectures on Shakespeare we understand him. When we read Shakespeare's dramas we, understand him but when we see the drama being enacted we definitely understand it perfectly and efficiently, this proves that eye is the most influential sense organ. This principle also holds good in praying also. Already we all exist in this world in some form, so we know the formlessness through form. It all boils down to—in the form, formlessness is present. It can also be explained further by saying, when you are playing a football game, you kick the ball, the ball gathers momentum and goes fast but it does not go automatically, it is you who make it go by exerting certain amount of energy or force. The very sight of the ball evokes and provokes your strength, your energy is released through some medium, but the strength is not there in the football but it is within you.

Seeing the idol of 'Linga' through such a cultured sense organ eye, listening to the idol of Mantra or Allah or the word or even noise through the sense organ ear, and chanting the idol of Shiva Mantra, through the sense organ mouth, smelling the idol of aromatic smell through the sense organ 'Nose' so creating an atmosphere charged with the divine spell of (Shiva) God through the five sense organs and becoming introvert meditating and praying to the God is the highest and an excellent and an effective kind of worship. Deficiency felt in the process of hearing while praying to God is made perfect when visualized as in the case of television, hence the deficiency is made more efficient and proficient.

The practices of the external world have created a conducive atmosphere for an intra experiences. In this way God has manifested himself in the five elements both in form and formlessness, that is why it is said "yatra jeevaha tatra shivaha" that is, where there is life there is God. Human being is in form, but when formlessness in him is realized then he becomes Jangama. The awareness with its formlessness becoming Jangama is being worshipped.

Every living being in nature is nurtured and fostered by nature and God. He is the cause of all existences, All the worlds are supported by a single wall, here the wall that keeps intact all the three worlds is not a mere physical entity but it is God himself who takes care of all the three worlds. This universe is supported by God for its independent existence. God keeps this world intact without causing any disturbance just like the wall which supports and posters all the portraits and photographs, which are hung on it. Here the wall acts, as benevolence and protector. All the photographs are in a finest condition in the protective and soothing cover provided by the wall. Similarly God too takes care of us and takes care of everything. He protects us he is our father. He is our supporter. He is the supporter of the whole universe. We all can feel the comfort in the lap of God, who is present everywhere in this universe. God is infinite as the sky and space are infinite. The sky or space cannot be measured. So also God cannot be measured. He is immense infinite and incomprehensible, abounding Gods grace sooths every soul in the nature and in the universe.

But the people of some religions perform the acts of charity only to destitutes and poor people. They feel that by their acts and deeds the God gets pleased but it is like feeding the son by his father and seeking pleasure for himself. Every object in the nature is a spark of divinity hence self-satisfaction is the real happiness.

Dasoha dharma or religion does not make any distinction or discrimination among the poor and rich, Sharanabasaveshwar a great, mystic soviet of 18th century lived the life of service, breathed service and his name is synonymous with service, because, he was of the opinion that work (physical) by body is a prayer to God. That is why sharanabasaveshwar never wrote any literature, as his life itself was a living fabric of literature, but he wrote through his service and certainly not through literature. His life and deeds have become a food for literary figures.

But the devotees read the literature of Sharanabasaveshwar (which was rather unwritten) through his rendering of service. So sharanabasaveshwar realized God not through writing but through the service. So his deciples also read God through the same service rendered by sharanbasaveshwar. They fulfill their dreams following his footprints. Hence the religion is not in the book. It is in their life. Life is in life only as it is the experience of the Upanishads "Yatra Jeevaha Tatra Shivah". So "Data Bhogata Swayam Shivah" That is, the one who grants is God; the one who receives is also God. That is why if the soul, which is in the form of man, is satisfied by all means, that is Dasoha or service and finally that itself becomes worshipping.

How is it possible to think and imagine of formlessness, when man himself is in form? We are reminded of formlessness only when we see a form. If it is formless, where is the question of worshipping? And how? That is why temples exists, statues are installed, the statues in the form are the symbols or representation of this formless life.

Letters that we use in our communication are only the signifiers but not the signified, hence the words are the symbols or signifiers of knowledge, but letters themselves are not the knowledge. As the clock is an instrument, which shows the time, but clock itself, is not a time. Here the clock is only a physical entity that reminds us metaphysical one *i.e.* from temporal to transcendental and physical to Meta physical. Similarly, Linga, Rudrakshi, Bhashma, Shabdha, Chanting of mantras are only instruments or rather means, which enable us to seek the God and show the God's abode. All the means or instruments used here have got a definite form but they display or help to visualize the objects of formlessness. Though a rose flower has a form, but its sweet fragrance is formless. Similarly among all five senses eye is supposed to be very powerful. This eye indulges in a very serious work. To attract the God through such a finest sense organ our elders made grand efforts to install the statues for the people. Our elders dreamed them to be the manifestation and emblem of God. Even Linga is the image or signifier of soul. Realization of God is a Sadhana, a spiritual journey, a constant endeavour and a craving of ceaseless spirit. It may either be an istalinga (worn on our chest) or Stavaralinga (installed deity) but the basic objective is the realisation of the form or swaroopa of our souls through them, is the real worshipping. Here we must be aware of the fact that, the concept of light originated because of the darkness, similarly the concept of formlessness originated from form. That is why either we need a Istalinga or Stavaralinga because form gets stimulated by form only "Bhavane illada Jeeva Alia" a life that is devoid of feelings cannot be called a life at all.

The people of different countries across the world use their own language as an instrument or a vehicle of thought to establish rapport or communication. Languages vary according to the region and the people. Although language seems to be externally as a means of communication if a thread bare analysis is made, it has much more serious jobs to do, a grand role to play. To throw further light on this aspect let us go further deep into the matter. Language is supposed to be most intricate and complex phenomenon developed by human beings across the world. There are hundreds and thousands of languages like English, French, German, Kannada, Hindi *etc.* but the verbal words used being attributed with certain sense and meaning to each word in all the languages carry the chord of communication with the accepted unarbitrary codes. But the codes have a limited role to play in human interaction, because the language used in communication cannot communicate completely as every communication is a half communication, because no communication can be perfect unless both involved in conversation come together talk together with mutual respect, love and kindness. Even we may use gesture, signs, pictures but they too have a limited role in the realm of language. Because what we express is not equal to what we experience, we may talk to a person for hours and hours and yet we remain strangers, in such cases, there can only be familiarity but not intimacy. Even the words used in every language are also a kind of vocal gesture or soundfull gesture or codes. Because the sound that is being produced at the time of uttering the word too has a limited meaning in a given context in a particular country. So the language of gesture may be understood in some countries but there is another language much useful and much higher than what we know in our own life, that lovely language is the language of love and service, the language of kindness, the language of affection, the language of devotion, the most universal in its appeal and nature. This very lovely language is spoken by Gods, so this tongue or language has to be adopted by one and all. Because this language has the power to divinise our lives, cement our relations, this language has the power to elevate our life, this very language has the power to take us to God. This language has the greater soothing effect, so let our language be more humanistic in its appeal, nature, mature enough, instead of being only dry with its codes. Let these codes, gestures and sound gestures be spruced with great love, affection, kindness and devotion, then there is no doubt that it will become an universal language, a language which could become more affable and would be most sought after. God reads language of devotees when it is a language of devotion.

As a dumb person establishes his communication with others non-verbally with the symbols or gestures; similarly language is also a product of such symbols and sound-gestures or vocal gestures (sanne swara). In this sense the very language that we use is also nothing but a gesture or a system of gestures. As already mentioned the language which is made up of artificial symbols and gestures needs to be infused with the feelings of love, affection and kindness, this alone could be a universal language. For instance when you call a child to come, it will not respond, if you call it with love and affection that subtle language definitely makes the child respond otherwise that language losses, its meaning and relevance. As a child responds to the language, which is pregnant and packed with love, affection and kindness, in the same way God responds to the language which carries the divine sparks of prestine devotion and pure and chaste feelings. God responds only to the language of Bhakti or devotion. That is why grand humility alone is the speaking God, here God responds to eternal and unweavering chaste love, this is the very language that makes God love you in turn, here when we give with chaste love that process itself is loving *i.e.* giving is loving, is giving joy and in turn that joy is loving.

To have the divine vision and realization of God, all the religions in the world have their own languages, they also have their own scripture, religions and their canons. Hindus posses Vedas, Upanishads, Vachanas, Puranas, similarly christens have their scripture *i.e.* Bible, Muslims have Kuran, the holy book and Buddhists have, Dhammapadas. In this way hundreds and thousands of books exist in different languages, against this background, we are prompted to ask a few questions like, which is the language of God? Which is the scripture that God reads? The irony is, God never reads any of these scriptures. The only language of God is the language of devotion, Bhakti, Kindness, love & humanity, well possessed in the hearts of the devotees. God never reads the books written merely with intelligence. God reads hearts of devotees, which are filled with love, affection, humanity, services and Dasoha. To be more precise, god reads devotion; he reads humanity, which are well brought in the book of a devotee's hearts.

Every plant, tree, creeper present in the nature are all a part and partial of the divine design of the God, accordingly they are all heading towards perfection and eternity, every act that takes place in nature goes towards ripening, purifying and maturity, which in turn guides man as lead kindly light in his endeavor to have a successful living. Everything that is present in nature grows; we all grow from boyhood to manhood, then become old. Then only life completes its full cycle of growth and maturity as the days go, time flies, the change of time makes man grow sweeter and sweeter but at an young age he is just like an unripe mango which is sour but as he grows older and older he becomes wiser and wiser, he also becomes ripe and mellow and also sweeter, just like a ripe mango becoming sweeter.

As stated earlier every plant, creeper and tree in nature aim at giving the mellowed fruit, eventually, which is their highest attainment in their lifetime. Similarly everything in nature grows older, ripes and finally falls down. As every tree ultimately aims at giving a ripe yield, similarly every living being in nature tries to have maximum pleasure, joy, and happiness in its life. Similarly man too aims ultimately to attain the stage of transcendentalism and eternal bliss in his life, which we call the Sachidanada swroopa. God who is after the divine souls, likes to have their company take away them as and when he wishes, it is just like this - as we wish for a ripe fruit and taste its sweetness, so also God wants to have those people who seem to be dearer to him and whose life has endeared him, it is just like a fruit falling down from a tree after a complete ripening, in the same fashion the human body, gets detached from the soul and falls down and in both the cases the acts are quite natural. Some people may die at an early age or at young age but they are just like raw and unripe mangoes, which are quite useful to prepare pickle, their early end in this world does not mean they are not dearer to God, they too are quite useful for certain occasions and jobs as unripe mango is used for pickle making.

So, their is no need to be panic about or scared of the natural act called death, which occurs on its own. When we consider that this body belongs to me 'I am the absolute owner of this mortal case,' then certainly we are chased by a terrible fear. Let us understand this truth with the help of an instance. When a child is given a doll, it gets immense happiness immediately, when the same doll is snatched away, the child begins crying, so here, crying is a sign of sorrow. When the doll is with the child that object belongs to child. In this way the feeling of possession becomes stronger. Similarly when the illusions like "this is my body, this is my feeling, this is my thought" are cherished, and then you are bound to be disturbed then the sorrow chases in the form of a devil. All the troubles and fears start when the feeling of possession is nurtured predominantly. Then the mind gets gripped by the fear more than that of a body, its impact is still much more on the feelings than the mind.

Normally everyone wants to get rid off this fear. But how to get rid off from it? What is the way out of it? Are the strong questions, which pester us. This way is the first and primary task of Dasoha Dharma and also the task of all realistic and practical religion.(Adenanu - Tadatme)

Man's enormous attachment in this world with his life and material wealth is indeed worthy of hundreds of stories. In life we are so much attachment to certain things that at some level, we just cannot think of living without these things. The rhythm of our life is so well tuned with these material and temporal objects that we pursue them with a feeling that this kind of life alone is a real one, alas! What a futile exercise man is making of? Man feels that his life devoid of things, which he loves most and adores most, is not life at all. He is an inalienable, inseparable part and partial of this worldly life-where he has a deep attachment and his roots are indeed very deep. Once I had a wonderful revelation of a profound truth of this saga of attachment. After all attachment for what? Is the seminal question.

Every year, I used to spend a some of Rs. Two lakhs for purchasing the Patroli leaves (which are used to serve the food) at the Dasoha Mahamane and I never used to feel for it as, these leaves were meant for the use and after the use they were just discarded or thrown away. Because the idea of throwing away the Patroli leaves was so well fixed and deep rooted in my mind that I never ever bothered for it. But the very next year I brought steel plates worth of 4 lakhs rupees thinking that they would last long instead of Patroli leaves. When these steel plates were used for serving food, plates worth of Rs. 4000 were lost. This indeed made me melancholic and sorrow full, because my expectation was proved wrong, it was falsified, I thought and contemplated over it again and again, it preoccupied my mind, I felt a sort of restlessness. This quench in me for truth led me into the wonderful world of profound truths of this great life. Because, though every year I used to spend Rs. Two lakhs. I never felt the loss as I had no attachment for patroli leaves, thinking that they are meant for use and there on disposed off. But when steel plates were brought with a feeling that they remains permanently, agony began because there was tremendous attachment, rupees out of two lakhs worth steel plates, about Rs. 4,000 worth plates were lost after serving the food, there by my mind immediately began depressing just only for Rs. 4, 000 loss, though there was a loss of Rs. 2 lakhs annually for patroli, although there was a saving of Rs. 1, 96, 000/- rupees.

My mind never bothered for Rs. 1, 96, 000 but only for Rs. 4000? What ails this mind, nothing but attachment, for meager of 4,000/- and detachment for 1,96,000/- attachment for less and detachment for more? What a strange humdrum of life it is? Here I realized the futility of attachment not to either more or less money but attachment to permanency.

Therefore we should realize that attachment to God is only real and eternal. So hold the one that is truthful and permanent but not the one, which is temporary. We must surrender to god serving him eternally alone brings us bliss with a felling that everything belongs to him, I am only a humble servant of God. Because service is another name for Dasoha. Dasoha is service and service is Dasoha.

A day will come when this when this body of ours will be used like the patroli leaves and later on it will be discarded, when I realized this profound truth of life, the sorrow nurtured and nourished well within me just disappeared. Even if death becons there is no fear only when we think this body is permanent like the steel plates, then we are bound to be hunted by the fear of death. So let us say "death be not proud; I have conquered you" and make a total surrender to God the almighty that alone knows how to take care of us. So we must hold that is truthful and permanent and not the temporal one to be in the divine company of God.

As happiness increases into many folds when a new car is brought in place of an old car similarly even our body also grows older and fragile and becomes over whelmingly happy feeling that it is entering into a new body.

When we are fleeing being gripped by the fear of body owing to the chasing of the dogs then we confront with a lion (mind), which terrorizes our mind. Then suddenly the fear of chasing dogs subsides but the fear of a lion increases. When we escape from the lion and the fear of it goes off immediately, then we confront with devil called death. At this stage the fear of lion extincts very rapidly but what a tragedy! Immediately the fear of death starts haunting. This is how the fear is very intense in the mind than in body, this very fear increases into many folds in our feelings than in our mind-this indeed leads to multiplication of our sorrows, here mind gives more pain than body, feelings give pains more than mind.

When we think deeply and dedicate our body to the God present in ourselves and realize that we are not meant for this body, then the fear of death will dispel and melts away and the same death becomes a grace abounding and a gateway to visualize the God and which in turn gives us a profound joy and bliss. At this stage one should have a feeling of floating, he should also realize that the eating stomach, worrying and mediating mind, and feelings and impressions of the sight-none of them belong to him.

This kind of feelings indeed endears him to God. God certainly seeks the company of such people, blessed are those who attain a celestial position and are in the divine company of God. If everything is attributed to God thinking that all this possessions belong to God, if lived, removing desire and enticement on them, then man is bound to live a peaceful, blessed life and all the obstacles called five senses like dog, lion and devils (i.e. body, mind feelings) will run away, so when we, offer this body to god it does not mean that we have lost it. It is a deed of nebulisation. It is a highest kind of activity that man can think of, dream of and perform it. When man has given them up and feels that he has really given them, and then they are there only, they are there in abundance.

As everything belongs to him only, when we offer we are reminded of that they belong to God. So we must keep offering everything that we have and keep remembering the God always.

Some religions in this world believe that there is a rebirth, some other religions declare and believe that there is no rebirth. Every object and living beings in this nature is subject to the cycle and process of birth, growth and death. This is the rhythm of life; one has to pass through all these stages. The purpose of the 'Life' that enters into a micro organism or a lowest level called insects to the highest level or macro beings including the highly civilized cultured and novelized human being-is to attain salvation. It is a means of liberation. This is the highest kind of happiness.

This is a supreme bliss it can also be a wonderful, rare and a unique opportunity or a destined occasion for the release or liberation of the life. If this opportunity is used in a right and proper way and lived fully for the cause that this life is meant for, then it means to say that it is an act of revelation or apocalypse. When this revelation is attained for people of this kind or this class or transcendentalism, this very life becomes the last one. It amply speaks of their soulful living, a complete living, a total living. Once the life is lived to its leese or brimful then it is indeed the last one. The life of human beings is a means or passage for growth, refinement and finally for salvation.

The process involved in seeking salvation finally can be easily understood if we look at the theory of evoluation of man propounded by Darwin from his most primitive stage to the latest development achieved in all dimensions of human activities from spiritualism to science. According to science, there is a evoluation theory, that science accepts evolution, science believes in the past for what man stands today, science also believes what would take place in future based on the present. From this it is quite clear that science accepts changes, change is the order of the day, change for the development. As the English philosopher Nitze says, there is a growth-taking place everyday. So from the above explanation it is quite valid and relevant to presume and accept that there has been a grateful growth, refinement and finally release or liberation from this body as well as the liberation from the attachment to the material life, or wealth. So, here release from attachment does not mean release not mearly from life but also from enticement at certain stage it becomes a passionate deed of life. We should realize that life has great opportunity of education, growth, and liberation. This can be compared to the life cycle of the plant. As tree is grown and nartured by watering, sunning and giving required dozes of fertilizer and pesticides, from a seed, the way how the plant grows out of a seed and attains a mammath size bearing leaves and flowers and finally giving the fruit, when the fruit becomes fully mellow and ripe which are relished by human beings, in the same way from micro insects to the macro level, say, human beings, when man becomes perfect and reaches the highest stage of salvation step by step, he can certainly merge with God and become one with him. But we should also bear in mind that though some fruits are mellow and yet they are not relished. They fall down before they are relished. So, as fruits grow in this form and content, similarly man grows in his form, that is in his flesh and blood. God desires these fruits, which are ripe and mellow.

So every organism in nature is heading towards perfection as every drop of water in river is ultimately, flowing rather journeying towards merging with sea. The last stage in the cycle of life of a tree is blossoming of flowers and bearing and yielding of fruits. Similarly the last and the final stage of an organism is becoming man himself or attain manhood. This human life is a means or passage to realization or self-actualization.

So when great souls like saints, seers, sharan's pass away or depart from this world, they are well received and given a grand welcome by none other than the God himself. The divine door of the God is ever kept open and is ready to invite such great souls, when the meeting of God and human `being takes place, it is indeed a celestial sight, what a rare event what a confluence when they meet, each merges into the other and they became one. This spiritual merger is what every one would seeks after.

So those people who are in contact with divinity, at this stage, such people have neither birth nor death. That stage is a stage of Swayambhu. That stage is a swaswaroopa merging with God. Or the stage of self-actualization. But those people who are not subject to this kind of stage have both rebirth and re-death.

Those who attain transcendentalism through realization can become Lingayath by revelation of God in life. Such people merge with Linga in their death.

> Lileyadade Umapati (Dasoha)
> Lile mugidade Swayambhu

Living in the divine and pious company of the realized souls and establishing divine contact and spiritual common with them is a path of Mahadasoha. That is why the Mahamane the abode of realized souls like sharanas is more holier than the visit to temple. Visiting such holy places itself is pilgrimage and a spiritual journey. Seeing their holy abode is a darshna or divine visualizing, receiving in such holy abodes of sharans is a sacrament and, the sublime canons of Dasoha (service) philosophy, are to triumph and transcend beyond both the birth and death, and this is Mahadasoha sutra. At this stage if we make efforts to seek God only in temples and churches it would be a futile exercise on a grand scale, because we can have the holy and pious glimpses of God in man in his very flesh and blood. God does reside in souls of human beings not in temples and churches built with bricks and concrete. God does live in temples in symbolic form.

It we want to learn a science lesson, we have to go to a science teacher. If one wants to become a scientist, he has to learn the nuances of science from scientist. In the same way if we want to unravel the mystery and understand the truth, God and pathway to God, we have to go to a teacher, a learned philosopher or realized souls, such divine souls teach us and unravel the truth and path way to God. If you want to become God and truth unto thyself then you have to pay a visit to those shivasharans whose life is a testimony of the transcendentalisms,who have become an embodiment and paragon of truth, those shivasharanas who have become God unto themselves or who have attained that God head. These are they very people who have intensely experienced what is the self-experience of God, these are the people who have profound and divine experience of God, and these are the people who have intoxication of God. Then, they also become the paragon of truth by establishing deep divine contact with the realized souls of shivasharanas whose spiritual wealth is a becoming light and they also become God by their own resplendent grace, which radiates from their magnetic personalities ceaselessly.

"There is a way of life prescribed among the Veerashaivas that called Dasoha and which, in a very real sense, is a study in excellence, Dasoha is a difficult word translate freely into English; it implies humility service, understanding, compassion, ıespect for one's fellow citizens, self abnegation, in fact a whole range of virtues with which we are familiar when Christ washed the feet of his disciples it was Dasoha.

When Christ fed the multitudes that had come to hear him, it was Dasoha. Dasoha is one when proclaims without any reservations that one is the servant of the lord and the lord is not someone up in heaven, but Lazarus at your doorstep the man in need, any man....Dasoha is excellence in cercelsis". So opines Sri. M.V. Kamath in his "The Pursuit of excellence".

Such an abode to truthful shivasharans is indeed greater and holier than vaaranashi, where as vaaranashi God is attributed. It is as good assaulting the portrait of the husband that too in his very presence. But this can never be equated to that. As the devotee of Godis God himself, thefore court of such a (shivashakti) devote is greater than Varanashi. Here, we have alive God; god living in his very flesh and blood, here the God is moving and walking. That is why here is a necessity of eternal Dasoha. The spirit of God, pervades every where and Dasoha is taking place there, so the thrust of our argument is that God entered intot his earth in the form of life.

There is a Dasoha in the total dedication of mind and feeling. Dasoha in action is the very love we have towards God. God is formless therefore serve your own self, which is a visible form of that invisible God. Pray and Serve the God by serving those, where there is life and where there are realized souls; Candle your light that is enlightenment, through there are many candles, but the light they emit is one. So keep performing Dasoha through the body, mind and soul. So, even writing and composing literature through which when the souls are made to realize their potential and the very presence of God in them is an outstanding form of Dasoha through literature. It is indeed a highest and an excellent form of service but it is one of the forms of service. Dasoha is-love in action to God.

Therefore, Dasoha siddhi is held by those who have the realization of God. Dasoha siddhi, is held by those who have become God and who are an emblem of deciation.

That is why going away for lakhs of miles to seek the company of bhakta or a devotee is sadachara. If you serve them through Dasoha or if Dasoha is performed to satisfy those devotees then Kudalasangama (God) himself will live and dwell with them. Dasoha sutra is nothing but the pristine and divine company of sharanas, serving the realized souls has come in the form of Dasoha sutras or the doctorines of Dasoha. The Dasoha philosophy has given us the gem like tenets to make our life self-realized, as self-realization itself is knowledge. As the soul alone is permanent and eternal, every thing what is visible is bound to perish. God is invisible, God is permanent, and hence he cannot perish. Therefore seek him through Guru, Linga and Jangam.

PART - II

DASOHA SUTRAS

by Poojya Dr. Sharnbasvappa Appa.

1

Maha Dasoha Sutra

The Lord himself
Came down to earth.
He became linga
By being static;
And then jangama
By moving;
He became guru
By knowing;
O friend,
Thus only by praying
To the Lord
As guru, linga,
Jangama,
Constantly,
Does one
Ultimately
Experience God.
That experience,
O friend,
Is Shivanubhava,
Knowledge of God.

What was Yesterday
Is History;
What is Today

Is Awareness;
What is Tomorrow
Is Yearning;
O friend,
Remembers,
Continuous
And constant
Be your Realisation.
That realisation
Alone
Is Realisation of God.
For God's messenger
Authority lies
In Scriptures
Received by Man.
But for the Mind
Awakened,
Authority lies
Not in Scriptures,
But in the Realised Life.

Thus, and for
That Reason
O friend,
Focus constantly
And ever
Thy mind on Shiva.
For, in the end
Awareness of Shiva
And Shiva alone
Is Awareness of God.

Says Mahadasohi Sharana Basava.

•••

2

Maha Dasoha Sutra

O friend,
I ask you
What is dasoha?
Listen:
That is dasoha
Which understands
The secrets of
TheVedas,
The Shastras,
The Agamas,
The Gita,
And the Puranas.
Know that that
Knowledge
Is dasoha.

What, friend,
Again, is dasoha?
Listen:
When you
Grasp
The core
Teachings of
Buddhism,
Jainism,

Sikhism,
Nirankarism,
That, friend,
Is dasoha.

Once again,
Friend,
What is dasoha?
Be aware
That in understanding
The significance
And inner meaning
Of Christ,
Of Zoroaster,
Of Mohammad,
Lies dasoha
Know, too,
That dasoha
Is what those
In the Great
Tradition of
Sharana Basava
Who studied
The vachanas,
And reaped the
Benefits of
Their association
With Basava
Realised in
Themselves,
And their conclusions.

Know Ye what
Has been said of Yore:
That all that

Surrounds us
Is the dwelling
Place of the Lore.

Thus is the world
A Temple
And the secrets
Of all religion
Truly is
Dasoha.

Therefore,
O friend,
For that reason
See the spirit of
Dasoha
In all that is
Around you.

That is dasoha
The universal
Religion.

Says Mahadasohi Sharana Basava

•••

3

Maha Dasoha Sutra

O friend
Let me tell you
What Kayaka is.
Kayaka is that
Which you perform
For the sake of dasoha.

Kayaka is that
Which you offer
To God, in prayer
In an act of
Selflessness
Where the self
Is subjugated
To the Lord.

Where you labour
O friend,
With zeal and
Devotion.
There, friend,
Laxmi dwells
In her splendour.
Where labour is
Performed

In the spirit of
Dasoha,
There, O friend,
Your offerings
Become worthy
Of Acceptance
By the Lord.

What one does for
Oneself
Is marginal
To life.
What one does
For others
Is the True Life.
What one does
For others as
An offering to God,
Now that, my friend
Is the dasoha
Of Kayaka

Says Mahadasohi Sharana Basava

•••

4

Maha Dasoha Sutra

O friend,
Did you hear
The Gurus,
Elders,
Mystics,
The Shastras
And the Puranas
All proclaiming
That the Lord
Dwells
In the Soul?

But, in the
Chanting of words
The meaning was lost,
In the emptiness
Of words
Realisation
Was lost.

But Basava
And others
Have pointed
The way out
Through
The dasoha sutra.

Said Basava:
Think of honeycomb
Built on sugarcane;
Can you fancy
The comb
Tasting the sweetness
Of the cane?

Even so
Said Basava,
Wealth, Life, Pride,
Keep man apart
From jangama.

Thus spake
The Lord of the
Confluence of Waters.

To weed out Pride,
Grant us
The dasoha
Dharma
Of Humility,
O Lord!

Where there exists God
There can be no Ego
Or Pride.
So they told us
To wipe Ego out,
But not to forsake
The World
Or Life.

So Siriyala
And Changale,
Basava and others,

Sharana Basava
And other Sharanas
Met Nirvana
The Lady
With their own wives.

So, O friend,
Acting without Ego
Is a sure way of
Destroying Ego.

Giving without Ego
Is dasoha
For it ends Pride.
And what is Prasada?
That it is
Which is received
Again without Ego
And Pride.

Remember,
O friend,
When you forget
Yourself
But forget not
God
Within you,
Reflected is
The Lord.

Such indeed
Is the sutra
Of dasoha

Says Mahadasohi Sharana Basava

•••

5

Maha Dasoha Sutra

Who is
Sharana Basava?

He is the one
Who taught
Dasoha

Who taught
How to give

Who taught
Giving is
The only true
Service,

Who routinised
The routine
Of giving,

Who taught
That wishing
Well to all
Living creatures

Wishing
Peace and
Well-being

And invoking
Dasoha in all,
He who
Invoked this
Sutra,
He is
Mahadasohi Sharana Basava

•••

6

Maha Dasoha Sutra

Serve guru, linga
And jangama
With body, mind
And all that you
Possess.

But only if
It doesn't occur
To you
That you have
Done so
Will you get
What you didn't
Even wish for!

So have
Basava and others
Sharanas
Said.

He gets
What he never
Asked for
Without asking
Who gives
Freed of

Ego
And prasada
Is what the
Gets.

It is this
Prasada
Which cleanses
You
Of karma
And endows you
With Eternal Bliss.

This is
The attainment
Of dasoha.

This truly,
Is the
Dasoha Sutra,
O Friend!

•••

7

Maha Dasoha Sutra

For the refugee
The guru is
His Refuge.

For the Refugee
The linga is
His Refuge.

For the refugee
The jangama is
His Refuge.

His salutation
Has nothing
Untrue about it.

Seeing refuge
Is true dasoha,
O friend!

Let your eyes
Themselves show
How deep your
Craving for refuge
Is.

That should suffice
To wipe away

The sins of
Your last seven births.
So the saints have said.

If only
Every refugee
Were to say
From knowledge
That God resides
In every soul,

In that knowledge
Lies
Shiva darshana,
Which is dasoha,
O friend!

•••

8

Maha Dasoha Sutra

To know
The Inner Resources
Of the Mind
Is Knowledge

That is
Our Guru

Let dasoha
Inform all our
Outer activities.

Can one
Do away
With ignorance
Without knowledge?

Can one
Do away
With darkness
Without light?

Knowledge
Imbued with
Submission
Turns into
Upanishads.

Similarly,
Knowledge
Imbued with
Submission
Becomes
Words of Wisdom.

Though
You may light
One lamp
With the flame

Of another,
The lamps may be
Many,
But the light
Is one.
It isVishwa sanskriti,
World culture.

Service
Through dasoha
Is Shiva prasada.

As the lights
Of Dipawali
Shine
May the
Awareness
That knowledge
Is guru
Shine
Throughout
The world

Says Mahadasohi Sharana Basava

•••

9

Maha Dasoha Sutra

The Upanishads say:
That your mother
Is God,
That your father
Is God,
That your teacher
Is God
That your guest
Is God.

That everything
Moving,
Stationary
Is God.
But the Sharanas say,
That greater
Than God
Is your mother;
That greater
Than God
Is your father.
That greater
Than God
Is your teacher.

That greater
Than Shiva
Is Shiva Sharana,
The one
Who has taken
Refuge in Shiva

And Basava said:

There's none left
But Me.

Forgetting himself
Immersed in Him
In devotion,
He saw
The whole world
Became jangama,
The moving god.

This, then, is
True dasoha sutra,
O friend!

Says Mahadasohi Sharana Basava

•••

10

Maha Dasoha Sutra

In my family divine
Husband is
Guru-linga-jangama
In the eight-fold
Home
Eternal,
Boundless,
Continuous
Love,
Is true bhakti,
It is dasoha.

Mantra, rudraksh,
Bhasma
Are my treasured
Ornaments,
In our togetherness.

For Shiva
Who lusts after
Devotion
My five-fold
Conduct is
Great attraction.

The get darshan

Of Lord Mahalinga
Through the
Nine Gates
Of the Body
Is the
Realisation
Of the Mystery
Of the nine lingas.

This four-fold
Approach to God
Is the essence of
Dasoha.

•••

11

Maha Dasoha Sutra

Sweet is marriage
But imprisonment is
Sweet relationship.

Sweet is marriage
And beautiful
Is the mingling
Of two bodies.

Friendship between
Two families
Can be rugged indeed.

Joyous is
The inter-action
Of two minds
Indeed.

Yet again,
Sweet is marriage
But imprisonment
Surely,
Is intimate relationship.

A relationship
Of two souls,
Mutually enriched

In Body and mind
Is soulful of delight.
The greatest joy
For a wife is
To see in her husband
The Lord Himself.

Similarly,
For the husband
To see in his wife
None other than
Mahadevi
Is a relationship
Of supreme Joy.

To see
In mutual well-being
One's own happiness
Is hardship indeed.

O friend!
Remember:
What is rightness
In marriage
Lies in
Seeing dasoha
In everything
Including
Regettiny a family.

•••

12

Maha Dasoha Sutra

Can a devotee of Shiva
Demolish a Shiva Temple?

Can a devotee of Vishnu
Demolish a Vishnu Temple?

Can a devotee of Jina
And Buddha
Demolish basadhis
And Viharas?

Can Christians
And Mahommadans
Demolish Churches
And Mosques?

Lord,
Demolish they can
The stones that go
To make the Walls
But not you.

There is only
One God for
All religions.

Names you have
Many
But in truth

You are one.
Destruction is
Wrought
Not for love
Of you
But in pursuit
Of man's own
Fanaticism.

Destroy nothing
Tear down nothing

Abuse not,
Nor cause pain
To others
By your harsh
Words.

The body which is
Greater than
A Temple
That is bestowed
By God Himself
Should not be harmed.

The Lord who lives
In that body
Should not be harmed.
To injure such a body
Is more of a sin
Than destroying
The temple of God.

Giving pain to
Pranajangama
That lives in
The body
Is worse than

Destroying the
Image of God
In a temple.

The sense of division
Exists
In the minds of
Man;
Nowhere else.

If you see
Yourself
In everything
Around you,
You will know
That differences
Exist only in
Our minds
Not elsewhere.

Even if you are
Hurt,
Hurt not others:
There in lies dasoha.

For the sharanas say:
The reason is
In not giving
And not receiving
Others are made happy.

Shedding ill-will,
Seeing God in all,
Creatures,
Desiting only good
For all:
That is dasoha.

•••

13

Maha Dasoha Sutra

Lingachara
Sadachara
Sivachara
Ganachara
Bhrityachara
These five-fold acts
Are five aspects
Of dasoha,
Myfriend.

Awareness of
Nothing else
Other than linga
In dasoha
And that is
Lingachara.
All activity
Ceaselessly done
In spirit of
Dasoha
Is Sadachara.

Seeing Shiva
In all living beings
Is dasoha

And that is
Shivachara.
And to hear not
Any insult to Shiva
That too,
Is dasahoa
Which is ganachara.

Considering
Shiva sharanas
As greater than
Shiva himself
And in that knowledge
Offering them
All you possess
In body and mind
Is dasoha
And it is
Brithyachara.

Practising
These five acharas
Always in the spirit
Of dasoha
Is the essence of
Dasoha dharma,
My friend.

•••

14

Maha Dasoha Sutra

What is there
In a mere idol?
So saying
People prayed
In open space.

But what is there
In open space?
So saying
Some built temples
And set up
Idols within
And worshipped there.

O Lord!
Since you're both
Form and Formless,
With and without
A form

Formless
Enlightment
In the form of body
Is worshipped
As jangama.

That formlessness

Installed in form
Is jangama linga
Which accepts worship.

So Basava
And other holy ones
Have said.

The ideal way
To worship is this:
It is
Attaining dasoha by
Seeking God
Through jangama.

•••

15

Maha Dasoha Sutra

There are many
Who insist
That re-birth is
Inevitable.

There are equally
Many who insist
That there isn't
Anything like it.

Many again say
That birth and death
Are what mark
A worldly man.

But Lord Basava said:

Our sharanas
Have neither birth nor death.

He also said:

If I take birth,
I'll lead a blessed life
Serving guru-linga-jangama
Receiving *thirth*.
And *prasad*.

As had been said:
Does it matter
Whether a sandalwood tree
Grows in a jungle
Or in a town?
Either way
Its fragrance
Stays the same.

When Shiva
Takes form on earth
It is as dasohi.

When he has to
Depart,
It is back to
Himself.

So his devotee
In life is
Immersed in
The linga

On his death
He returns again
To the linga.

Here in action
On earth
He is Uma's Consort

The action
Over
He is swayambhu
Self-born.

Thuswise,
In the illustrious

House,
Where a sharana
Does his dasoha
Holier it is than
A Temple to Shiva
Himself.

Wherefore
The journey to
That House
Becomes a
Pilgrimage
And sighting
A sharana
Becomes a
Vision
And receiving
What is given
Becomes
Prasad itself.

Conquering the
Chain of Birth
And death,
That is the
Essence of
Dasoha,
My friend.

•••

16

Maha Dasoha Sutra

What is the difference
Between worldly
And otherworldly
Concerns,
My friend?

What is meant by
Sharana wife
And linga husband?

The bond with a wife
Is love.

The bond with children
Is belonging.

The bond with kinsfolk
Is friendship.

When the bond with
Teachers, elders, God,
Is made, fully worthy
Of Trust,
It is transformed
Into the dasoha
Of Bhakti.

When the Bhakta's devotation
To dasoha

Is unwavering
The bhakta becomes
Maheshwara.

When Maheshwara's
Unwavering devotion
To dasoha
Gets focused,
He is prasadi.

When the prasadi's
Devotion to dasoha
Gets enlightened
He is pranalingi.

When pranalingi's
Devotion to dasoha
Combines with
Divine bliss,
Then he is Sharana.

When that Sharana's
Spouses' devotion
To dasoha
Fuses with linga
Husband,
Then he is *aikya*.

Since the dooer
And the activator
Are the same;
Since all
Practice is
Endowed with
Dasoha bhakti

Know then
That this is
Shatsthala dasoha.

•••

17

Maha Dasoha Sutra

I tried talking
To you.

It was like a
Dumb man
Expressing himself
Through hand-signs.

My sound-signs
Could have been
The sounding
Of a conch.

Attempting to
Talk to you,
I stood as if dumb.

Listening to me,
Was it like
An elder being
Annoyed
At the sound of
Children banging
On the drums?

Language is
But a vehicle;

It is not God.
The one language
To speak with God
Is bhakti dasoha,
God's only tongue.

Be Jyotirlinga
Through wordless
Talk.

That is the Way
Of Mahadasoha
Which sees
Without eyes
Like the Three-Eyed One.

•••

18

Maha Dasoha Sutra

Frightened was I
Like a man
Chased by a dog
When I thought
This body is mine.

Frightened was I
Like one faced
By a lion
When I thought
This mind is mine.

As I considered
Myself, imprisoned
In my thoughts,
The darkness deepened
My terror of death
Appeared as a ghost
To torment me.

But before the dog
And the lion
And the ghost
That is death
Could touch me,
I offered my body

To Ishtalinga,
My mind
To Pranalinga
And my thinking
To Bhavalinga.

Whereupon
When I felt
Chased by a dog,
I felt the presence
Of the lion,
And lost the fear
Of the dog.

Even so,
When I felt chased
By a lion,
I felt the presence
Of a ghost,
And lost the fear
Of the lion!

And were the ghost
That is Death
To chase-me
In the darkness,

In the light of
Bhakti dasoha
Death would are
And darkness
Lie exposed
Naked to the eye.

When Death dies
It becomes
The Great Door

To God,
Mahanavami, no less.

Living this
Fierce bhakti,
I became
Shiva Himself.

And, like a plant,
A tree, a vine
That bring forth
In turn,
First flower,
Then fruit,

Even so
Life should ripen,
End
In Truth, Beauty
And Bliss.

That is
Dasoha's Way,
Says,
Mahadasohi
Sharana Basava.

•••

19

Maha Dasoha Sutra

To understand
The ways of God
One must
Follow the guru.

To understand
Kudala sanga
One must be
Among the sharanas.

Holier than
Deva Loka
The abode of Gods,
Is the home of
The Shiva bhakta.

Holier than
Varanasi
Is the courtyard
Of the Shiva bhakta.

Holier than
Mount Kailas,
Is the body of
The Shiva bhakta.

Wherefore

The wise ones say:
Forbidden
Is earthly pilgrimage.

True pilgrimage
According to them
Is the pilgrimage
To the sharanas.

That is sadachara
That seeks
Companionship
Of Shiva's bhaktas,
Even if one
Has to travel
A hundred thousand miles
To be with them.

And with them,
If you serve,
Yours is God,
So say the wise.

Fellowship
With the sharanas, then
Truly is
The essence of dasoha.

•••

20

Maha Dasoha Sutra

What, O friend, in *Kayaka*?
That which is done without ego
That which is done with devotion
That which is done with
Total concentration of mind
That is Kayaka.

And what is dasoha?
That which is given without ego
That which is given with devotion
That which is given with
Single-mindedness
That is dasoha.

And what is *prasada*?
That which is received with devotion
That which is received in tranquility
That is *prasada.*

Whatever is done
In total devotion
Without pride
Without ego
Becomes *Kayaka.*
Becomes worship.

Any devotion
Accompanied with pride
Leads to karma.
Not even worship
Can truly prevent it.

If what you earn
Is given for the happiness
Of all Living beings
With total devotion
Then it is true *dasoha*.
Such a one
Attains salvation

Remember,
The Lord descends on earth
As *linga* being static
As *jangama* through movement
As *guru* in bestooing
Enlightenment.

It is this trinity
Of Guru-linga-Jangama
That is one
Without a second.

Follow then,
The five-fold conduct:
Be pure in your daily activities
Wear the *linga* on your body,
Serive for the establishment
Of Saivism in your surroundings
Be dutiful to your colleagues
In this enterprise
And serve all devotees
Birth humility

Thereby
Through the smearing
Of ashes
Through wearing
The sacred rudrakshi
Chain
And through
The chanting of
Right *mantras*
Once attains *dasoha*
That, friend,
Is the essence of *dasoha*.

This alone is
True
And the devotee who
Understands this
Truth
And worships
Without ego

Strives without attachment,
Offers without attachment
And received without
Attachment
Acquires prasada
The gift of God
Such a one
Indeed is *linga*
The presence of God.

•••

21

Maha Dasoha Sutra

Uniting body with God
Through the nine-foldpath
Is the essence of *dasoha*.

Thus wise flesh is
Transformed into
Mantra,
The invocation to God
Becoming the Gift of God

Despise not
What is bestowed
To the body:
So has said Basava.

Remember:
No saint has forbidden
Sexual pleasure as such.
For from pleasure
Truth can be realised.
Even as from sour butter
Ghee can be realised
And from food
Strength can be realised.

It is in offereing
Everything to God

In the highest
Can the cleansing
Of Body and mind
Be realised.

And what, pray,
Is *Prasada*, Tranquillity,
The Gift of God?

Serving God
Through the objects of
Sanctified smell
Sanctified taste,
Sanctified touch,
Sanctified sight,
Santified sound
All contentment
Sanctified
Because it is dedicate
To God
Becomes prasada
The gift of God.

Wherefore,
Surrender
Everything
That is yours
In Heart, mind and wealth
Fully and totally,
In the service of the Lord
Without reserve,
In full detachment
With no claim that
Anything is yours
Thus wise, attain
Dasoha

Says MahadasohiSharanabasva

PART - III

TRANSLATION & COMMENTARY

by M.V. Kamath

Mahadasoha Sutra

The Lord Himself
Came down to earth.
HE became linga
By being static;
And then jangama
By moving;
He became guru
By knowing;
O friend,
Thus only by praying
To the Lord
As guru, linga,
Jangama,
Constantly,
Does one
Ultimately
Experience God.
That experience,
O friend,
Is Shivanubhava,
Knowledge of God.

What was Yesterday
Is History;
What is Today
Is Awareness;
What is Tomorrow
Is Yearning;
O friend,

Contd....

Remember,
Continuous
And constant
Be your Realisation.
That realisation
Alone
Is Realisation of God.
For God's messenger
Authority lies
In Scriptures
Received by Man.
But for the Mind
Awakened,
Authority lies
Not in Scriptures,
But in the Realised Life.

Thus, and for
That Reason
O friend,
Focus constantly
And ever
Thy mind on Shiva.
For, in the end
Awareness of Shiva
And Shiva alone
Is Aswareness of God.

Says Mahadasohi Sharana Basava.

Sutra - I

In the firmament of contemporary philosophers the name of Poojya Shri Sharana basavappa Appa stands out as a shining star. A scholar and spiritual leader of no mean repute, Shri Appa is a unique figure whose contribution to Sharana literature has endeared him to his followers.

His latest contribution is in the nature of twenty-one Mahadasoha Sutras, naturally in Kannada which are of exceptionally high literary merit. Even more importantly their spiritual content stands out as a beacon to the searcher after Truth. They are, needless to say, entirely in the tradition of Vachanas originally popularised by the Veerashaiva Mystics with the 12th century onward.

The most commonly accepted meaning of the word ' vachana' is: the spoken word.

That which is uttered. But in Veerashaiva literature the word assumes a much higher meaning. Associated with it is a certain spiritual halo that distinguishes it from ordinary wisdom.

The Vachanas of Basavanna are a class by themselves. Unlike Sankara or Madhwa, Basava composed his work in Kannada, the language of the people. Like the Buddha before him, Basava's desire was to communicate with his fellowmen in a language they could understand and relate to. The vachanas speak directly to the heart, which is why they have a special place in Kannada literature.

Shri Appa's mahadasoha sutras are in that same noble tradition. They are written in Kannada and therefore have a special appeal to kannadigas. The English translation is intended for a larger audience.

A word about Mahadasoha Sutras. "Dasoha" is derived from the original Sanskrit words: dasa and aham. In essence they mean: "I am the servant". (dasa = servant; aham = I am). In dasoha, as Shri Appa has mentioned it in another context, the onus is entirely on doing, on action, on one's total involvement in compassion.

The word sutra, again in Sanskrit, means 'thread'-that, which connects. It is also defined as the basic principle of a subject arranged for study. In Pali, the word becomes sutta and thus we have Sutta Nipata, The Teachings of Buddha.

Mahadasoha Sutra, in effect, means the principle whereby the seekar breaking the barriers of caste and creed, rank and position identifies himself with all living beings, a condition as Shri Appa himself explains it "of universalition of oneself and of cosmic at-homeness".

In the course of the sutras reference is made to such words as linga, sthavara, jangama wich again call for explanation. The word linga is understood in Veerashaivism to mean the highest Godhead, the Transcendant Truth, the Final Reality or the parabraman. It is not to be confused with the dictionary meaning which is phallus. Linga, or God, is the union of para-Shiva and para-Shakti. As one distinguished Veerashaiva philosopher and savant has put it: "It is the mass of the ineffable Light, the mine of the inscrutable Bliss, the matrix of the innumberable words. It is the real entity and ever existing joy which is eternally perfect.

The word linga is derived from the root gama, meaning to go deep, to penetrate in, to comprehend, as in the case of adhigama or the more familiar word in Kannada, gamana. But how does one get to comprehend the incomprehensible? How does one comprehend God, the Ultimate Reality? Is that possible for mere man to under go that transformation?

Yes, avers Poojya Appaji. The Lord can be comprehended. Why? For the simple reason that he comes down to earth, as linga, a sign, a mark, or a symbol. In the Upanishads, the word linga is invariably used in the sense of a mark or a symbol.

avyakteshu parah purusho vyapako linga yeva cha
No cheshita naiva cha tasya lingam
Mahadadyam vishesantam lingam

most of us need something tangible to focus our minds on. It is all very well to say that the nirvikar, formless, which is static the obvious. The ordinary mind can't focus on nirakar unless one is in deep meditation. So one needs a form, a shape to pitch in our attention. Hence the need for a sign, a mark or a symbol. For the Veerashaivas, the linga marks the symbol, just as, for Christians, the Cross is the symbol. Just as Christians wear the cross on a chain round the neck for a Veerashiava, wearing a linga on one's person becomes the hallmark of the true devotee.

The Veerashaiva sees god in everything, in things that are static, as in things that keeps moving, in fact in all creation. There is God in every movement. Jangama is anything that keeps moving, life itself. Derivatively a jangama is a saiva sanyasin who can be a teacher, a guru. And a guru has claims for attention. Rightly has it been said:

Gurur brahma gurur vishnu
Gururdevoh maheshwara
Gurursakhshat parabrahma
tasmai guruveh namah

In the true guru one sees the Lord himself and to that guru one must bow down in reverence. So we have here what Poojya Appaji mentions in his very first stanza: the static linga, the moving jangama and the guru who is the teacher. It is in praying to them, he says, that one ultimately experiences God-Shivanubhava.

Shivanubhava-experiencing Shiva or god-calls fir continuous yearing. Realisation does not come to one who is insincere or unwilling to seek. As the Bible says: Ask and it shall be given unto you; seek and ye shall find, knock and it shall be opened un to you. Everone that asketh receiveth; and he that seeketh, findeth. So one seeks God, regularly.

Deligently, humbly. The scriptures help insofar as they bring the message of God to Man. But the aim should be to go beyond the Scriptures towards an understanding of oneself which calls for deep and sustained introspection. For it has been said: "In the light of the lamp the defect of the lamp is seen; by looking at a mirror, the defect in the eye is found. Therefore one should realise oneself through oneself". That is exactly the point made by Poojya Appaji.

In this guru can help. The guru culfils two functions:

- He gives conceptual knowledge, notably what the search should be all about and
- He makes the disciple, the seeker, think for himself.

The teacher does not offer authority; what he provides is guidance. (As. J. Krishnamurti used to say: "Together we are going to seek, find, discover the right answer") The Kathopanishad put it this way:

Sahanavavathu
Sahanavbhunakthu
Saha viryam karavavahai
Tejasvi navadhithamasthu
Ma vidvishavahai

(May the Lord protect us both-teacher and the taught-together. May he strengthen us together; may he enliven our dialogue; may there be no differences among us). In essence the guru must help the seekar to focus his mind on Shiva-the Reality. What is this Reality-this Shivanubhava? (Sir Ramana Maharshi said: "Brahman (the Reality) is not be seen or known). It is beyond the three-fold relationship of seer, sight and seen, or knower, knowledge and known. The Reality...is neither light nor darkness but heyond both".

Then what is it?

It is eternal search. Poojya Appaji says: "Focus constantly and ever they mind on Shiva. Awareness of Shiva and Shiva alone is Awareness of God".

That dasoha
Is what those
In the Great
Tradition of
Sharana Basava
Who studied
The vachanas,
And reaped the
Benefits of
Their association
With Basava
Realised in
Themselves,
And their conclusions.

Know Ye what
Has been said of Yore:
That all that
Surrounds us
Is the dwelling
Place of the Lord.

Thus is the world
A Temple
And the secrets
Of all religion
Truly is
Dasoha.

Therefore,
O friend,
For that reason
See the spirit of
Dasoha
In all that is
Around you.

That is dasoha
The universal
Religion.
Says Mahadasohi Sharana Basava.

II

Mahadasoha Sutra

O friend,
I ask you
What is dasoha ?
Listen:
That is dasoha
Which understands
The secrets of
The Vedas,
The Shastras,
The Agamas,
The Gita,
And the Puranas.
Know that that
Knowledge
Is dasoha.

What, friend,
Again, is dasoha?
Listen:
When you Grasp
The core
Teachings of
Buddhims,
Jainism,
Sikhism,
Nirankarism,
That, friend,
Is dasoha.

Once again,
Friend,
What is dasoha?
Be aware
That in understanding
The significance
And inner meaning
Of Christ,
Of Zoroaster,
Of Mohammad,
Lies dasoha
Known, too,

Contd….

Sutra - II

This Sutra is intended to define what dasoha in all about. What in effect, is dasoha? Where does it begin and where does it end? How is one to apply it, in one's day-to-day life?

The first thing to do says Poojya Appaji,is to understand the scriptures and go beyond the words. For behind the words lies wisdom. The commanding word in this sutra is: Know. Know what the Vedas, the Upanishads, the Shastras, the Agamas, the Gita and the Puranas have to say. Keep an open mind. Read them carefully, Digest their thoughts. Get to the core of the teachings of mystics and philosophers, and try to understand the significance, the inner meaning of Buddhism and Jainism, Sikhism and nirhankarism, of what Christ, Zoroaster and Mohammad have to say, and what the great tradition of sharanaasavais all about.

That Poojya appaji is asking is for the seeker to eschew dogmatism, for when the mind is shut to other ideas, growth gets stunted, as well. God is everywhere so is truth. The problem is to find it without prejudice in all religions. Says Poojya Appaji:

Know ye what has been said to yere; that all that surrounds us is the dwelling place of the lord. Thus is the world a Temple.

One is reminded of what kabir said:

He is apart from the universe, yet the universe is in him; such a lord do I serve, there is none apart from him.

Again;

Where do you seek me, O friend
I am right at here beside you;
Nither in temple nor in mosque am I
Not in kaabaa nor kailas
Nor am I in rites and rituals

Nor yet in yoga or renunciation.

Shri appaji catholicity is clear in his advice. He does not reject any religion out of hand, nor does he demean the prophets and saints. His advice is: Be aware. Find out the "inner meaning" of every religion; go to its core. Then one can't go wrong. Shorn of all the outer trappings, Shri appaji is only too aware, all religions have the same message. It is going to the core of all things, now that, he says is dasoha.

Most of the tensions that arise in world is for lack of dasoha. The propagators of some religions make it a point to assert that they, and they alone have the Truth. That their Scriptures alone hold the key to eternal life. Shri Appaji has no such pretensions. The seeker does not go for labels. He is free. When the whole world is a Temple, when all religions ultimately have to lead to the One and Only, where is the place for dogmatism? For "We" and " They"? For the true Seeker, all belong to the same family. All are "We". There are no "They". That again, is dasoha. The Brahadaranyaka Upanishad says as much:

> "It is only in duality that one can see another, speak of another, think of another, know another. Where everything has become the Self itself, whom and by what should one think? By what can we know the Universal Knower?

When one speaks of dasoha- I am the servant-the question legitimately arises: servant of whom? The answer should be obvious. One is the servant of all mankind. It is in the service of mankind that one becomes a servant of God. And to serve mankind one does not have to wear saffron or grow a beard or look solemn. The social worker in the slum, the doctor in the poor man's hospital, the nurse in the leprosy home, why, even the grocer round the corner does his bit for mankind. The trick is to detach oneself from one's deeds. The Gita says:

> Karmanaivadhikarasthe ma phaleshu kadachina

Your duty without clamouring for the fruits thereof. Serve for the sake of service . Albert Schwitzer went to the jungles of

Africa to serve the tribals in Congo he not looking for some one to recommend him for the Nobel prize, When Acharya Vinobhha have undertook his bone-shaking paadayatra, his aim was not to get Bharat Ratna but to serve the poorest and the lowest. Jnaneshwar has made the same point in his Karma-Marga:

> If one who has given up all desires to engage in any activity, engages in the practice of samadhi, is not that practice also an activity, and why should not he who has his occupation have also the activity of the family?

In other words to be a dasohi one does not have to be a sanyasi. Dasoha is not something exotic that can be taken on hand only by the sanyasi. The practice of dasoha is open to all, at all levels and is not exclusivist. The Yoga Vasistha says:

> Just as the bird is able to fly by virtue of its two wings so too (by means of) both janana and karma is obtained the enduring Brahman.

Shri Appaji puts this thought beautifully. He says:" See the spirit of dasoha in all that is around you. That is the universal religion".

(There is universality in service.) Service is not exclusivist. It is not confined to one people, one race, one class or one religion. The great Basava was, is and will for ever remain a model. He was beyond caste and creed. He spoke to and for all mankind. And that is the core of this sutra.

Dasoha, however, is not confined to service as we know it, alone. That would be simplifying the concept. Dasoha embraces other fields like Knowledge. To know is also to serve.

Dr C.V. Raman, the Nobel Prize winner, once said:

Science is nothing but a search for truth-Truth not only in the physical world, but in the world of logic, psychology, behaviour and so on. The virtue of a truly scientific frame of mind is the readiness to reject what is false and untrue. It proclaims from the housetops that there is no virtue in sticking to untruth. I think the latest biological discovery is that there is no fundamental cleavage between the life of man and the life of the lower creation and that salvation lies in the perfection of the biological instinct-the instinct to sacrifice the individual for the same of the species.

Contemplate some of the things Dr. Raman has said: Reject what is false and untrue. Life is one. Be ready of the sacrifice of the individual for the greater good of the many.

Dasoha is expressed in many forms. This is Gandhiji's interpretation of what true service is:

> The true devotee (the seekar) does not hate or bear ill-will to any living creature. He looks on all with love and compassion. He is free from the delusion of 'I'and "Mine". He reduces himself to zero. Pleasure and pain are equally acceptable to him.
>
> He dedicates his intellect and mind and all to him. He
>
> is free from exultation and sorrow, anger and fear. He seeks nothing for himself. Although he is firm in his resolve, he is indifferent as regards the success and failure of his action.
>
> He moves freely as if he is alone...

Without knowing it, perhaps, Gandhiji was expressing the spirit of dasoha. Whether it is Dr. Raman, Mahatma Gandhiji, Dr. Radhakrishna, Swami Vivekananda, they have theirown interpretations. But in all cases, Shri Appaji's exhortation holds good. Listen to them all.But go beyond their words to the inner core of their thought there lies dasoha.

III
Mahadasoha Sutra

O friend :
Let me tell you
What Kayaka is.
Kayaka is that
Which you perform
For the sake of dasoha.
Kayaka is that
Which you offer
To God, in prayer
In an act of
Selflessness
Where the Self
Is subjugated
To the Lord.
Where you labour
O friend,
With zeal and
Devotion.
There, friend,
Laxmi dwells
In her splendour.
Where labour is
Performed

Contd...

In the spirit of
Dasoha,
There, O friend,
Your offerings
Become worthy
Of Acceptance
By the Lord.
What one does for
Oneself
Is marginal
To life.
What one does
For others
Is the True Life.
What one does
For others as
An offering to God,
Now that, my friend
Is the dasoha of Kayaka
Says Mahadasohi Sharana Basava.

Sutra - III

This is a short sutra but it is full of meaning.

Poojya Appaji concerns himself with the definition of kayaka. It can be defined in one short word: Action. But that would hardly do the term any justice. Poojya Appaji seeks to define it in many enlightened ways. Thus: Kayaka is that which you perform for the sake of dasoha. It is that which you offer to God, in prayer and an act of selflessness. It is that which you do with zeal and devotion. It is that which you do for others Kayaka involves selflessness, devotion care and love for others, concern for the welfare of the world, surrender to the will of God. Basava has described Kayaka as Kailasa,the summit of excellence, the last world in devotion, the attainment of godhood, In the Gita it is said:

Karmanaivadhikarasthe ma phaleshu kadachina

Do your work without desiring the fruit there of. The command is that one must be detached from one's actions. In giving, one should not expect to get anything in return. Duty is an end in itself. It is only when one gives freely, unreservedly, in an act surrender that the gift becomes meaningful. Give in the spirit of dasoha, advises Poojya Appaji, so that one's offering is worthy of acceptance by the Lord.

Selfishness is natural to man. When we give a donation to a temple, a school or a hall, we would like our names to be inscribed in letters of gold so that all the world would know what we have given. We seek name, frame, glory. It gives us great satisfaction that our gift is recognised, that we are known to be benefactors. We fool ourselves into thinking that we have done something for others. That, alas, is just not true. What we have done is for our own self aggrandisment. That is not what is meant by 'giving'. "What one does for oneself" says

Poojya Appaji, "is marginal to life. What one does for others is the True Life". And what one does for others is not meant to be trumpeted, written about, praised. It is to be done in the secrecy of one's heart. Let not they left hand know what has been done by the right hand, says the Bible. That is true giving.

True giving implies sacrifice and self-purification. A principal of a National College once wrote to Gandhiji critising him, for one of his articles in Young India that extolled sacrifice". Your article on sacrifice is nearly heart rending" wrote the Principal, " you seem to be expecting more sacrifice from those who are willing and have already done their best... "By way of reply Gandhiji wrote: In the first instance there can be no limit to one's sacrifice. A sacrifice that calculates and bargains is hardly sacrifice. In the second instance, one does not ask from or expect anything from pretended followers. They do so not under compulsion but voluntarily and joyfully. And, at the end of the giving, they regret that they have not given more".

To give voluntarily and joyfully and to regret, at the end giving, that one had not given more is, in a sense dasoha. In giving there is no end. What one does for others says Poojya Appaji is True Life. It is also true love. Says the Bible: " Greater love hath no man than this, that a man lay down his life for his friends". That is the ultimate in love, as in life. It is that giving which is acceptable to God.

There are many among us who do social service. We work in the slum or give our time for the uplift of the under privileged or to assist the lame, the blind and the dumb. But how much of this is serving for the sake of service? And how much to be seen, to be taken notice of, to be praised, to hope that in due course one would be awarded with at least a modest Padma Shri? In working for an award we, in marginalise ourselves.

Serving others for its own sake is not drudgery. It becomes drudgery when we hate what we do. We must serve because in service we see the face of God. Service should not be an act of atonement either. It should be free, spontaneous, without any desire attached to it. In giving one should forget the 'I' when one gives in the true spirit of dasoha, there is no 'I' nor is there the 'other' The 'I' and the 'other' cease to be. In everything that we do we only see God. The Yoga Vasishta puts it in another way: It says: The distinction between 'I' and 'you' is imaginary. The distinction between the one and the many is verbal. All these do not exist at all even as darkness does not exist in the sun. On enquiry all these disappear and only the unmodified pure consciousness remains".

What we give should be total, one cannot hold back, It is expressed most beautifully in the following lines:

Kayena vachaa manasendriyayva
Buddhyatmana va prakrithey swabhavat
Karomi yadhyatsakalan paraswai
Sarveshvaryethi samarpayami

All that I do by word, deed, senses nature or through inspiration, indeed, whatever I do, it is an offering to God in total submission, it becomes worthy of acceptance by God who alone knows what is in our minds. We can cheat ourselves, but we cannot to cheat God.

Life becomes meaningful only when service is above self, when service is indeed not seen as a service but as an act of dedication. Enlightenment comes when one forget a that one is the 'doer', when one remembers that one is merely an instrument, the conduit, what the Gita says is nimitta matra. Significantly enough, today's management experts teach that excessive concers about results interferes with the efficiency of activity!

That is Karma Yoga in action!

And that is what this sutra is all about. Even Shakespeare has something to say about true giving. " Love sought is good, but giv'n unsought is better!" It is in giving that we receive.

IV

Mahadasoha Sutra

O friend,
Did you hear
The Gurus,
Elders,
Mystics,
The Shastras
And the Puranas
All proclaiming
That the Lord Dwells
In the Soul ?
But, in the
Chanting of words
The meaning was lost.
In the emptiness
Of words
Realisation
Was lost.
But Basava
And others
Have pointed
The way out
Through
The dasoha sutra.
Said Basava:
Think of a honeycomb
Built on sugarcane;
Can you fancy
The comb
Tasting the sweetness
Of the cane ?
Even so
Said Basava,
Wealth, Life, Pride,
Keep man apart
From jangama.
Thus spake
The Lord of the
Confluence of Waters.
To weed out Pride,
Grant us

Contd...

The dasoha
Of Humility,
O Lord !
Where there exists God
There can be no Ego
Or Price.
So they told us
To wipe Ego out,
But not to forsake
The World
Or Life.
So Siriyala
And Changale,
Basava and others,
Sharana Basava
And other Sharanas
Met Nirvana
The Lady
With their own wives.
So, O friend,
Acting without Ego
Is a sure way of
Destroying Ego.
Giving without Ego
Is dasoha
For it ends Pride.
And what is Prasada ?
That it is
Which is received
Again without Ego
And Pride.
Remember,
O friend,
When you forget
Yourself
But forget not
God
Within you,
Reflected is
The Lord.
Such indeed
Is the sutra
Of dasoha
Says Mahadasohi
Sharana Basava.

Sutra - IV

Ask your gurus, your elders, mystics, the Shastras and the Puranas where God is: and the inevitable answer will be: He resides in the Soul, We leave it at that. We have the answer. The scholar may even recant the mantras to show that he knows all about where God is. Isn't he in the soul? What more needs to be said?

This is where, Poojya Appaji says, we get lost. In the chanting of the words, the meaning is lost. In the emptiness of words, realization is lost. To option realization we have to go beyond words, to understanding.

The Brihadaranyaka Upanishad syas:

"Where there is duality, there one sees another, one smells another, one tastes another, one speaks to another, one hears another, one knows another; but where everything has become one's own self, with what should one see whom, with what should one smell whom, with what should one taste whom, with what should be speak to whom, with what should one hear whom, with what should one touch whom, with what should one know whom? How can he be known by whom all this is made known? He, the self, is not this. He is ungraspable, for he is not grasped. He is indestructible for he cannot be destroyed. He is injured. Indeed by whom should the Knower be known? Such, in truth, is immortality." To achieve Realisation, then, one has to know the all pervasive feeling of duality. That there is 'I' and there is the 'Other'. And from that certain knowledge one must take the next step: the conquest of 'I".

It is easy to say that we must conquer the 'I' the Ego but how can this be done? The first step, of course, is to be humble, to forget oneself, to see God in every living being, to give without desiring the fruit of our action. In the precess we have to give up our pride and our sense of self-importance. It is pride that makes us conscious of ourselves. It is when we forget ourselves-when we give up our aham-that we open ourselves to the grace of God.

But can we attain this state without forsaking the world? Yes, we can. There is a common misconception that says that one must forsake the world, become a sanyasi, in order to conquer oneself. This is a completely wrong idea and Lokamanya Bal Gangadhar Tilak actually wrote his Gita Rahasya to refute this belief.

One can be Enlightened by being part of the world and by acting in a detached manner. Says the Gita: "Unattached to the fruits of action, he does what needs to be done, he is the one who has truly renounced, and who is a true yogi, and not he who relinguishes all action".

And the Yoga Vasishta says: The knower has nothing to gain either by performing or by abstaining from action. There fore, he performs action as (the need for it) arises". Therefore the way to enlightenment is not to renounce life and action, but to live and to act. Janaka, the Wise, was a king. Janardhan Swami, the guru of Eknath, was killedar (commander of a fort) and Nisargadatta Mahara, continued to sell bidis in his small shop! There is wisdom in work, which is offered to God. The Zen poet P and Miraculous power and marvelous activity.

Drawing water and hewing wood!

The enlightened man may go unnoticed even by those nearest him. In the words of

Entering the forest he moves not the grass
Entering the water he makes not a ripple

This is the quality of naturalness sought to be conveyed by the term *Sahaja sthithi* which is used to describe the state of Liberation.

It is not acquiring wealth that leads one away from God; it is not acquiring power that leads one away from God. It is not the acquisition, but the *manner* of acquisition that is the root of all trouble. And all acquisition should be an act of dedication; it should be considered as *prasada*, that which is received, without ego, without pride. In his classic work *The Vedic Experience*, Raimundo Panikkar in discussing Karma Yoga writes:

> Lord Krishna, in the Gita, certainly does not preach abandonment and neglect of one's duties or the merely mechanical performance of one's action. He does not preach that we should do things without enthusiasm, passion and ideals. On the contrary, he permits no flinching or easy-going interpretation of each man's proper dharma. Nevertheless he insists that all actions must be done with a pure heart and detached mind, with the sovereign freedom that is the fruit of the univolved spirit and preserves the distance which is necessary for a proper perspective.
>
> Committed, not as casual stranger, yet detached and univolved, not as a slave; this how the Lord in the Gita asks that we should perform all human action.

Poojya appaji speaks of the dasoha Dharma of Humility. Where there is Humility, action reduces itself to dedication to the Lord. The fruits of that action, in turn, is received as *prasada* that which is given, again in dedication to the Lord. Neither the action nor the fruit really is ours. They both belong to the Lord.

This is true Unmility.

Our actions, then should be like building a honeycomb on a sugarcane. Can one fancy the comb tasting the sweetness of the cane? Even so, should our action be in the field of action. They are independent of each other.

> Not by rituals and resolutions, nor by much learning, nor by celibacy, not even by meditation can you find the supreme, immortal joy of nirvana, until you have extinguished your self-will.

And that is what Poojya Appaji says: "To weed out Pride, grant us the dasoha Dharma of Humility, O Lord!"

That is the core and content of this sutra.

V

Mahadasoha Sutra

Who is
Sharana Basava?
He is the one
Who taught
Dasoha
Who taught
How to give
Who taught
Giving is
The only true
Service,
Who routinised
The routine
Of giving,
Who taught
That wishing
Well to all
Living creatures
Wishing
Peace and
Well being
And invoking
Dasoha in all,
He who
Invoked this
Sutra,
He is

Says Mahadasohi
Sharana Basava.

Sutra - V

Who is Sharana Basava?

Basava is a historical figure. Sharana Basava lives amongst us. He is with us all the time. He is one who gave the mantra of dasoha. As was explained in Sutra1, dasoha in effect means "I am the servant". A servant, in effect, serves. He serves impartially, seeksing no regard. To give and continue to give is his life's mission. The akshays patre of love is bottomless. Thee more one gives the more still remains in the vessel.

Giving is loving; and the reverse is equally true: loving is giving. It is not just giving. The Latin meaning of charity is dearness, the being dear, being loved. The root word is caritas. It is in the sense of loving, loving beyond all calls of duty that is the essence of dasoha. That point was raised by Christ's disciple, Pual in his first epistle, letter to thee Corinthians. It is appropriate to quote him. He told the Corinthians:

> Though I speak with the tongues of men and of angles, and have not a Charity, I am become as sounding brass or a tinkling cymbal. Thought I have all faith, so that I could move mountains and have not charity, I am nothing. And though I bestow all my good to feed the poor and though I give my body to be burned and have not charity, it profiteth me nothing. Charity suffereth long, and is kind; Charity envieth not, charity vaunteth not itself, is not puffed up; Doth not behaveth, itself unseemsly, seeketh not her own, is not easily provoked, thinketh no evil. Rejoiceth not in iniquity, but rejoiceth in the truth. Beareth all things, believeth all things, hopeth all things, endureth all things...

Poojya Sharana Basavappa Appa has put it in a different way. Giving he insists is " the only true service". Wishing all living creatures well, he avers and invoking *dasoha* in all is the true service. *Dasoha*, he might have said, is the untimate. Even if one could move mountains, even if one offered oneself in sacrifice, but without the spirit of dasoha, it amounts to nothing.

Sages down the centuries have said much the same thing, if in different ways. Service, to be truly effective, indeed to be truly service, has to be disinterested. It should seeks no profit; it should bear no desire. The Buddha said: "Do not fail to do what ought to be done. Otherwise your burden of suffering will grow heaviest". For the dasohi there is no suffering; therefore there is no burden to carry. He asks for nothing; he gives because giving, loving, is part of his inner being. In giving the rejoices.

Pual stresses the force of charity, love, again and again. There things abide, he has said: Hope, faith and Charity. But he adds: "But the greatest of these is Charity" because "charity never faileth"

"Wishing peace and well-being and invoking *dasoha* in all " that is the message of Poojya Sharanbasavappa Appa. Now who can challenge that? Wishing the well being if all studes not just human beings or friends and relatives and strangers, but all living beings without discrimination. Implied here is nonviolence, *ashimsa. Ahimsa* as our sages have said, is paramo dharma. Non-violence is the greatest of laws. And nonviolence, again, not just in action. Non-violence has to be observed in though, word and deed. The mind must be pure, and so should be the heart. Let us go back to the Buddha again and to *Dhammapada:*

> They are not following dharma who resort to violence to achieve their purpose But those who lead others though non-violent means, knowing right and wrong, may be called Guardians of the dharma. Dharma is upheld by living in harmony with it even if one is not learned. One is not noble who injures living creatures. They are noble who hurt no one

Mind the word *harmony*. A dasohi by definition lives in harmony with everyone and everything around him. He is first of all at peace with himself. Inevitably he is at peace with all around him, whether man or beast, friend or foe rich or poor. To a *dasohi* there is no scope for differentiation between the one and the other. He sees God in everyone.

It is not easy to be in harmony with others, unless one is at peace with oneself. That, indeed, is the secret of good living, of inner happiness. To be at peace with oneself, one must first sacrifice one's ego. The 'I' becomes unimportant. The 'I' merges with the universe. When that happens harmony automatically prevails.

The true *dasohi* is ever willing to merge with the world around him. The Self for him ceases to exist. He is part of all. And when that is understood, what else is there to be understood? The Mundaka Upanishad said it all in these glorious lines:

> Yatha nadhya syandamanh samudre
> Astam gachchanti namarupe vihaya
> Thatha vidwan namarupad vimukhtah
> Paratparam purusham upaiti divyam.

(As flowing rivers go to rest in the ocean and there leave behind them name and form, goes to that divene Man who is beyond the beyond, higher than highest, transcending the transcendant).

(when one practices dasoha, he is like the river that has joined the sea, leaving behind his ego, his self and everything else. His love joins the ocean of love. The one becomes the many.

Being a dasohi is to attain the highest form of being. As it has been said, loving is being. And loving is giving. And giving is serving.

VI
Mahadasoha Sutra

Serve guru, linga
And jangama
With body, mind
And all that you
Possess.
But only if
It doesn't occur
To you
That you have
Done so
Will you get
What you didn't
Even wish for!
So have
Basava and other
Sharanas
Said.
He gets
What he never
Asked for
Without asking
Who gives
Freed of
Ego
And prasada
Is what he
Gets.
It is this
Prasada
Which cleanses
You
Of Karma
And endows you
With Eternal Bliss.
This is
The attainment
Of dasoha.
This truly,
Is the
Dasoha Sutra,
O friend !

Sutra - VI

This is one of the most beautiful sutras. It calls for what is generally described as nishkama karma-selfless duty. It is entirely in line with what the Bhagavad Gita says. In the krishnarjuna samvad (chapter II) Krishna tells Arjuna:

> Karmanaivadhikarashhe
> ma phaleshu kadachhna
> mate sango ' stva karmani.

(you have a right in respect of action (work) alone, never in respect of its fruits. Let not the fruit of action be your motive and let there be no attachment to inaction either)

Now this has to be read in conjunction with several other recommendations made in the *Gita* such as:

> yogastha buru karmani
> sangham tyaktva Dhan anjaya
> siddhi assidyoh samo bhutva
> samatvam yoga unchyate

(oh Dhananjaya, renouncing attachment and being unmoved alike in success and failure, do your duties firmly entrenched in yoga (means of knowledge). This state of equanimity is called yoga.

Further:

> Karmajam buddhiyuktaa hi
> Phalam tyaktva manishnah
> Janma bandhava vinir muktah
> Padam gacchantyanaamayam

(Those who renounce the fruits of karma surely become possessed of God and get liberated from the bondage of birth, reach the goal free from suffering") *Sutra 6* says that one must serve guru, linga and jangama with body, mind and all that one possesses. There are no ifs and buts here. One has to give up everything without exception and one must dedicate oneself completely, body, mind and soul and one mustn't even think that one has done so, for in just the very act of think-ing that one has given up one's possessions, one betrays one's attachment to possess-ions!

The Gita further says:

praxjahati yadaa kaamaan
sarvaan paartha mono gataan
aatmanyevaa tmanaa tushtah
sthithap ra jnyadtado chyate

(when one gives up all the desire of the mind and, by the grace of God is content (finds satisfaction) in Him, then he is considered a God-centered sage capable of directly perceiving God.)

We may consider it *prasada*, the gift of God. It is the *prasada* that cleanses one of all karma and endows one with eternal bliss.

The path cannot be smooth. To free oneself of Ego cannot come easily. The body desires happiness of all sorts. The mind, mischievous as it is, hope from one stage of desire to another. The sage has said:

mana vemba markatava thadeyalarenu deva!

Lord, says the dasa, I can't withstand this monkey of a mind! can't indeed.

kshurasya dharaa nishitaa dhuratya
durgam pathastath kavayo vadanti

To walk on the path of righteousness is as hard as walking on the razor's edge. And yet that is the only way to receive the gift of *prasada*.

Wher. the *sutra* says that one must serve guru, linga and jangama in totality, it says in effect that submission to the guru must be total without any qualification. The mind must be free from anxiety and pain, indifferent amid pleasures, loo sened from passion, fear and anger. And why, it may be asked. The answer comes clear in the Gita:

Dhyayato vishayampumsah
sanghasteshupajayate
sanghat sanjayate kaamah
kaamant krodhobhi jaayate
krodhab havati sammohah
sammohat smriti vihrahmah
smritibrashmshadbuddhinasho ho
buddhinashaat pranashyati.

(who ever muses on the objects of the senses, develops attachment to them; from attachment springs up desire; and from desire arises anger; from anger results delusion or error of judgement; from delusion, loss of memory such as scriptural commandments and injunctions; from shattered memory there will be loss of good sense and understanding and when that happens one is certain to perish) so what is the answer? The Gita comes through clearly:

Raagadevesha viyuktaistu
vishayanindriyairshcharan
atama vashyairvidheyatmaa
prasadamadhi gacchati

(one the other hand, he who with the sense free from likes and dislikes and kept under perfect control and whose mind is disciplined, attains purity of mind and tranquility.) That is the prasada to which reference is made in the sutra. It is when the mind is finally cleansed of karma that one finds Eternal bliss. This, in effect, is dasoha.

One final definition of dasoha:

duhkeshvanudvignamanah
sukheshu vigatatasprohah
vitaragabhayakrodha
sthithadrirmuni ruchyate

(he whose mind remains unperturbed in sorrow and he who is devoid of longing for pleasures and is free from passion, fear and anger-surely he has attained dasoha)!

What the *sutra* does is to state the wisdom of the Gita in simple, easily assimilable form so that even the illiterate can understand and be motivated by it. That is the sutra's special significance and relevance.

VII
Mahadasoha Sutra

For the refugee
The guru is
His Refuge.
For the Refugee
The linga is
His Refuge.
For the refugee
The Jangama is
His Refuge.
His salutation
Has nothing
Untrue about it.
Seeking refuge
Is true dasoha,
O friend !
Let your eyes
Themselves show
How deep your
Craving for refuge
Is.
That should suffice
To wipe away
The sins of
Your last seven births.
So the saints have said.
If only
Every refugee
Were to say
From knowledge
That God resides
In every soul,
In that knowledge
Lies
Shiva darshana,
Which is dasoha,
O friend !

Sutra - VII

"For the refugee, the guru is his refuge. For the refugee the linga is his refuge. For the refugee the jangama is his refuge" says the sutra. For all of us the guru, the linga and the jangama are our refuge. Why? Because, in truth, we are all refugees. To believe otherwise is to fool ourselves. In the battle for life, in the battle for sheer survival we need a refuge. When we are down and out, when we are sad and depressed, when we cannot face the many problems that daily confront us, refuge. We need and who else can give it than the guru, the linga and The jangama?

To seek' refuge is to surrender. And when one surrenders one does not make it conditional. The surrender is total and voluntary. The Buddhists put it in another way. They have their three venerations:

> Buddham sharanam gacchami
> Dhammam sharanam gacchami
> Sangham sharanam gacchami.

In an insecure world they are a source of strength.

> I take refuge in enlightenment
> I take refuge in the eternal Law
> I take refuge in the fellowship of virtues.

Buddhism is a religion of hope. It extends protection to those in distress, provided they seek refuge and shelter in the Three venerations. Even so shri Poojya Sharanabasavappa appa says there is hope if one surrenders to the three sharana venerations: Guru, linga and jangama. The guru is the living reflection of the linga and jangama; he is the embodiment of hope; he is the one who can dispel doubt, extend hope and strengthen faith. It is through him that one is led to Linga and jangama, the ultimate.

The concept of seeking refuge is ancient. The bible says
O Lord, my god, in thee do 1 take refuge (Psalm 7)

over and over again, the psalmist seeks refuge in God. Psalm 11 makes the point even more strongly:

In the lord I take refuge,
How can you say to me,
"Flee like a bird to the mountains;"
But the wicked bend the bow...

Then again in psalm 16.

Preserve me, O God, for in these I take refuge...
Thou dost show me the path of life
In thy presence there is fullness and joy

And why is the psalmist so anxious to take refuge in god? It is because in surrendering to the lord he knows he gets peace and strength. This is broughtout forcefully in psalm 23:

The Lord is my shephered. I shall not want.
He makes me lie down in green pastures,
He leads me beside still waters.
He restores my soul.
He leads me in paths of righteousness
For his neme'sake.
Even though I walk though the valley
Of the shadow of death

I fear no evil.
For thou art with me;
They rod and they staff
They comfort me.

He who seeks refuge is never turned away. Seeking refuge, says the sutra, is true *dasoha*. In seeking refuge, one submits. And in submission, all one's sins are forgiven. One attains peace. This is stated in another way in the *Gita*:

apporyamnamachalaprathishtam
samudra mapah pravishanti yadvat
tadvat kamaa yam pravishanti sarve
sa shantimapnothi na kama kami

(Just as waters flow into the ocean which, through being filled on all sides, yet remains steady, all objects of desire enter him who is steady and it is he who attains salvation; not he who goes hunting for pleasures).

Here the guru is compared to the mighty ocean. The ocean is vast; it is steady; it accepts every drop of water that comes to it, and the waters at last find refuge in the sea. The simile is apt. When we go to our guru with all our multiple problems, our angers, our desires, our hurts, the guru does not turn us out. He accepts us. And in accepting us, he gives us peace.

The sutra says-and it is to its everlasting credit that it puts the thought in the simplest of words:" Let your eyes themselves show how deep your craving for refuge is". The eyes are the windows to our soul. The eyes reveal more than any other part of the body. When a person says that he wants refuge, only the eyes show the depth of his sincerity. The eyes betray the strength of his surrender, his willingness to accept succour.

In the end we go back to the Gita which says towards the end:

manmanaa bhava madhakto
sarvadhamaan parityaja
madyaji mam namaskuru
maam ekam sharanam vraja
mam evai shyasi satyam te
aham tvaam sarvapapebhyo
pratijaane priyo si me
mokshayishyaami maa subhash

(Fix your mind on me, be my devotee, sacrifice to me, prostrate yourself before me. You will reach me alone, this is true. I promise you, you are dear to me.

Having given up all duties not pleasing to me, come to me only as your refuge; I shall liberate you from all sins, be not grieved".)

And that is exactly what the sutra says in the language of the common man.

VIII

Mahadasoha Sutra

To know
The Inner Resources
Of the Mind
Is knowledge.
That is
Our Guru.
Let dasoha
Inform all our
Outer activities.
Can one
Do away
With ignorance
Without knowledge?
Can one
Do away
With darkness
Without light ?
Knowledge
Imbued with
Submission
Turns into
Upanishads.
Similarly,
Knowledge
Imbued with
Submission
Becomes

Contd….

Words of Wisdom.
Though
You may light
One lamp
With the flame
Of another,
The lamps may be
Many,
But the light
Is One.
It is Vishwa sanskriti,
World culture.
Service
Through dasoha,
Is Shiva prasada.
As the lights
Of Dipawali
Shine
May the
Awareness
That knowledge
Is guru
Shine
Throughout
The world
Says Mahadasohi Sharana Basava.

Sutra - VIII

In his work The Rock, T.S. Eliot raises an important question. He writes:

> Where is the Life we have lost in living?
> Where is the wisdom we have lost in knowledge?
> Where is the knowledge we have lost in information?

But what is knowledge? Is it merely information? Eliot asks: "Where is the knowledge we have lost in information?" Ergo, Eliot does not equate information with knowledge. The simple answer would be: what is known, is knowledge. But once again we come to the simple question: what is it that has to be known that is not information? The Chandogya Upanishad says:

What one performs with knowledge, with faith, with meditation, that indeed, becomes more effective.

Let us go back to the Gita:

> Shraddhavanlabhate jnaanam
> tatparah samyatendriyah
> jnaanam labdhvaa paraam shantim
> achirenaadhi gacchati

(He who has faith, is devoted to Me and has secured mastery over his senses, obtains that knowledge and having got it, attains quickly moksha.)

Indeed Chapter IV of the Gita is almost entirely devoted to the defining of what knowledge is. The subject is further explored in the Maitreyi Upanishad:

> Only by a tranquil mind does one destroy all action, good or bad.
> Once the self is pacified, one abides in the Self and attains everlasting bliss.

If the mind becomes as firmly established in Brahman as it is usually attached to the sense objects, who then will not be released from bondage?

> The mind has been declared to be of two kinds: pure and impure.

It becomes impure when it is touched by desire and pure when it is freed from desire.

When a man having made his mind stable, free from attachment and confusion, enters upon the mindless state, then he attains the supreme abode.

Only so long must the mind be controlled, until it is annihilated in the heart: this truly is knowledge, this is liberation.

In Chapter IX of the Gita, the lord further tries to educate Arjuna on what knowledge is:

> idam tu te guhyatamam
> pravakshyaamy anasuyave
> jnanam vijnana sahitam
> yajjnatatvaa mokshyasesubhaat

(To you who are devoid of the carping Spirit, I shall communicate knowledge of God combined with the most profound secret of knowledge by knowing which you will be free from evil)

And what is that "most profound secret of knowledge"? It is knowing oneself. It is, as this *sutra* states right from the beginning, "Knowing the inner resources of the Mind" which is truly liberating.

Just as one's guru teacher enlightens us on our duties and responsibilities, so does knowledge liberate us from our earthly bonds. But knowing oneself does not free us from our duties and responsibilities. He who is grown in knowledge does not run away from life. He continues to perform, selflessly. "Et *dasoha*" says the *sutra* " inform all our outer activities".

A clear distinction is made of activities. They are of two kinds: inner and outer. The outer activities are those we are engaged in as long as we live. They include work, study eating and drinking, struggling to keep alive, serving others and being served in return. The *sutra* lays down that all these outer activities must be carried out in the spirit of *dasoha*. It is only then that we are freed. But the inner activities are of a wholly kind and are carried out at another level.

The inner activities are a search for who one is and that takes effort.

The outer activities are important, even necessary. They must be performed. But they must be performed in the spirit of *dasoha*. The *sutra* says: knowledge imbued with submission becomes words of wisdom"-in other words, true knowledge. And service through dasoha becomes "Siva prasada".

One may define 'siva prasada' as Grace; one may even define it as liberation. It is attained through *dasoha*, through submission. In the Gita, the Lord says, submit to Me.

manmanaa bhava madhbhakto
madyaaji maam namaskuru
maam evai shyasi satyam
pratijaane priyo si me
sarvadharmaan parityajya
maam ekam sharanam vraja
aham tvaam sarvapaapebhyo
mokshayisyaami maa suchah

(Fix your mind on me, be my devotee, sacrifice to Me, prostrate before me. You will reach Me alone; this is true, you are dear to Me. Having given up all duties not pleasing to Me, come to Me only as your refuge. I shall liberate you form all sins be not be grieved.)

That, in essence is Siva Prasad.

The sutra ends with a blessing. "As the rights of Deepavali shine, may the awareness that knowledge is guru shine throughout the world". That is also a prayer. Be a Light Unto Yourself, says the Bible. It is our duty to spread that awareness of what true knowledge is, like one lamp lighting another and yet it the same one light that illumines life.

IX
Mahadasoha Sutra

The Upanishads say:
That your mother
Is God,
That your father
Is God,
That your Teacher
Is God,
That your guest
Is God.
That everything
Moving,
Stationary
Is God.
But the Sharanas say,
That greater
Than God
Is your mother;
That greater
Than God
Is your father
That greater
Than God
Is your teacher.
That greater
Than Shiva
Is Shiva Sharana,
The one
Who has taken
Refuge in Shiva
And Basava said:
There's none left But Me.
Forgetting himself
Immersed in Him
In devotion,
He saw
The whole world
Became jangama,
The moving god.
This, then, is
True dasoha sutra,
O friend !
Says Mahadasohi Sharana Basava

Sutra - IX

The Upanishads say:

> Matr devoh bhava
> Pitr devoh bhava
> Acharya devoh bhava
> Athithi devoh bhava

(Your mother is your God, your father is your God, your teacher is your God, your guest is your God). And behind that is the admonition: treat everyone as God., even the one who comes to your unexpectedly.

But the Sharanas go a step beyond. They say: Greater than God is your mother; greater than God is your father, greater than God is your teacher" but then the Sharanas go one step further: They say: " Greater than Shiva is the one who has taken refuge in Shiva!" That, now is a profound thought. Can anyone be greater than God? How can that be? This is where comes the power of submission. In submitting to Go, one makes God not the Master but! Incongruous though it may sound-the slave of him who submits!

That is a stupendous concept. God, the Sharanas say, has no alternative but to submit to one who submits to him! How can God turn away the refugee, who comes to him in total submission?

When a child submits to its mother, does the mother turn him away? When a child submits to its father, does the father push him away? When a student does to his teacher and says: teach me, can the teacher turn him out? Even so, when so, when a man goes to God and say: accept me, does God have any álternative but to accept him who has come to his door? Who, then, is the master, who the slave?

In the *sutra* Sharana Basavappa Appa makes an important

point on the power of submission. Submission is not servility. Submission is surrender. Strange through it may sound, when one surrenders to God, one in effect conquers God! That is the beauty and strength of surrender. God, in effect, is the servant of his servant!

This raises the concept of surrender to entirely new heights. Surrender to God is not a loss but a distinct gain! Basava says: "There's none left but Me"! He says: "Come to me". And he who goes to Him, gets his suitable award. Only he who goes to Him must go in the spirit of *dasoha*, seeing God in the whole world, in everything that moves, in service to the least.

As Charist out it: "In as much as ye have done it unto one of the least of these my brethren, ye have done it unto me!"

When the devotee sees the whole world as god and whatever is moving within it and serves all, in the spirit of *dasoha*, without his even being aware of it, he is one with Him, the one without a second!

X
Mahadasoha Sutra

In my family divine
Husband is
Guru-linga-jangama
In the eight-fold
Home
Eternal,
Boundless,
Continuous
Love,
Is true bhakti,
It is dasoha.
Mantra, rudraksh,
Bhasma
Are my treasured
Ornaments,
In our togetherness.
For Shiva
Who lusts after
Devotion
My five-fold
Conduct is
Great attraction.
The get darshan
Of Lord Mahalinga
Through the
Nine Gates
Of the Body
Is the
Realisation
Of the Mystery
Of the nine lingas.
This four-fold
Approach to God
Is the essence of
Dasoha.

Sutra - X

To understand the immensity of this sutra, one must know what is meant by

(a) Guru-Linga-Jangama (b) the six-stage bhakti (c) the eight-fold varana, (d) the five-fold conduct (*panchachaara*) and finally (e) the nine doors of the body.

The *sutra* starts with the simple assertion that guru linga-jangama is husband. Now, guru-linga-jangama together stand for Siva, the Lord Ergo, the relationship between the devotee and Siva would be analogous to the relationship between a wife and a husband.

And what is the six-stage *bhakti* (devotion)? The ultimate in devotion is attained, it is claimed, through six stages: through *shraddha* (diligence), nishta (unwaveringness), avadhana (intentness), *aubhava* (enlightenment), *aananda* (beatitude) and finally *samasara*, (absoluteness).

Sri Ramakrishana Paramahansa has often been hailed as a supreme example of one committed to devotion. He could, during his prayers, reach heights of ecstacy as can easily be discerned from his pictures. Devotion is a powerful instrument. There is the story-possibly apocryphal, but one nonetheless with a great moral of Kanaka dasa who wanted so desperately to see the face of Shri Krishna in the famous temple at Udupi. Belonging, as he did, to a low caste, he could not enter the temple. Nor could he get a glimpse of Shri Krishna from outside, as a well kept him out of sight. But Kanaka Dasa was not to be put off. He prayed. He sang songs of devotion to his god with total devotion. In the end, it is claimed, Shri Krishna Himself was moved by the power of Kanaka Dasa's devotion and turned his head towards the devotee. Stunned, the temple authorities carved out a window in the wall so that Kanaka

Dasa could feast his eyes on his Lord. It is appropriately called *Kanaka Kindi* or Kanaka's Window. A statue is now raised at the spot where Kanaka must have stood to sing praises to his Lord and Master. Kanaka, it is only fair to say, fulfilled all the six stages of devotion. In his singing there was diligence. In his praise of the Lord, he was unwavering.

God listens to his devotees. One way to God is *bhakti marga*. The devotee surrenders himself completely to God without any reservations. As Sankara would have said:

> I do not make any gift nor do I practice meditation. I have not read scriptures nor chanted hymns or *mantras*. I know not how to worship and possess no dispassion. In Thee is my only haven or refuge, in Thee are my help and my strength!

Kanaka Dasa says:

> Deshadhipathi narahariye ninnaya paadha
> Daasara daasanendu yenisabekenna

(Oh Lord, consider me as the servant of the servant of your feet!)

Shiva, says the *sutra* lusts after five-fold conduct-*panchaachaara*.

They include: (a) wearing a linga on the body-lingaachaara (b) being pure in one's daily activities *sadaachaara* (c) striving hard for the establishment of the order of Saivism sivachaara (d) being dutiful and responsible to the team of Saiva devotees *Gannaachaara* and finally (e) serving the devotee with devotion *bhrityaachaara*.

The eight fold Varana (*ashraavarana*) consist of the following: sacred ash that is smeared all over the body (*bhasma*) (d) the wearing of the *rudraksha* a seed considered holy © the chanting of the name of Siva as *mantra* (d) acceptance of the religious teacher as guru (e) the wearing of the *linga* (f) the serving of the *jangama*, the living Saiva saint (g) the washing of the feet of the guru-linga-jangama as *paadodaka* and (h) finally the acceptance of the gift given by the *gur-linga jangama* as prasaada.

The nine doors of the body are the five organs of sense-nose, tongue, eye, ear and skin, together with the personal god (*Ishta linga*) worn on the body, the subtle form of linga (*praana linga*) worn on the inner body and the subtles from of linga (*Bhaava linga*) worn one the innermost part of the body.

Nine lingas are identified: (1) Achaara linga (2) Guru linga (3) Siva linga (4) Jangama linga (5) Prasaada linga (6) Mahaalinga (7) Nishkaala linga (8) Nisshunya linga and finally (9) Niranjana linga.

These are nine aspects of god. Poojya Appaji says that to get the Lord's darshan, one has to go through the nine gates.

The devotee has to conduct himself well in his day-to-day activities. He has to adhere to truth and non-violence. He shall not lie or otherwise misbehave. In every way he has to be above reproach. He has to treat his *guru* as god, and be worthy of receiving prasada from jangama.

It is when the devotee understands the endlessness, eternity, indestructibility of God that he becomes worthy of God's grace and understands His Mystery.

And that, says Poojya Appaji, is true *Dasoha*.

XI

Mahadasoha Sutra

Sweet is marriage
But imprisonment is
Sweet relationship.
Sweet is marriage
And beautiful
Is the mingling
Of two bodies.
Friendship between
Two families
Can be rugged indeed.
Joyous is
The inter-action
Of two minds
Indeed.
Yet again,
Sweet is marriage
But imprisonment
Surely,
Is intimate relationship.
A relationship
Of two souls,
Mutually enriched
In Body and mind
Is soulful of delight.
The greatest joy

Contd...

For a wife is
To see in her husband
The Lord Himself
Similarly,
For the husband
To see in his wife
None other than
Mahadevi
Is a relationship
Of Supreme Joy.
To see
In mutual well-being
One's own happiness
Is hardship indeed.
O friend !
Remember:
What is rightness
In marriage
Lies in
Seeing dasoha
In everything
Inc luding
Regretting a family.

Sutra - XI

Sutra XI is a paen of praise for the institution of marriage but Poojya Appaji wants the couple to see more in it than mere intimate relationship. He wants the woman to see in her husband the Lord himself; at the same time he wants the husband to see in his wife "none other than Mahadevi". It is this relationship, he aver alone can bring "Suprme joy" to both. He wants each partner to see in the happiness of the other "one's own happiness". Shakespeare spoke of marriage in similar terms. One of his sonnets goes as follows:

Let me not to the marriage of true minds
Admit impediments. Love is not love
Which bends with the remover to remove.
Oh no! It is an ever fixed mark,
That looks on tempests and is never shaken.
It is the star to every wandering bark
Whose worth's unknown, although his height be taken.
Love's not Time's fool, though rosy lips and cheeks
Within his bending sickle's compass come;
Love alters not with his brief hours and weeks,
But bears it out even to the age of doom

The institution of marriage is as old as man himself. Marriage is a cosmic act that involves the whole universe. Several are the hymns devoted to the subject. In the Rg Veda the institution is described as damapti (house holder, lord of the house) which suggests a certain equality between husband and wife. As the Rg Veda puts it:

(Husband and wife in sweet accord)
give milk oblations to the Gods
Devoted to sacrifice, gathering wealth
They serve the immortal and honour the gods
United in mutual love

The stress is on "sweet accord" what Appaji talks about as the mutal enrichment in body and mind in the spirit of dasoha. The stress is on seeing dasoha in all actions, including begetting a family. In a discourse on the subject of marriage, pujyashri Chandrashekarananda Saraswati Swami of the Kanchi Kamakoti Pitha splet it out. A wife, said the savant, is called dharma-patini as also yajna-patni. She has to be with her husband in he pursuit of dharma and has also to be a source of encouragement in it. As a dharma-patni she has to be by his side during the performance of sacrifices; she must also play a supportive role in all those rituals that have the purpose of making the divine powers favourable to mankind. The relationship between husband and wife is aatmic, not just physical. There were three samskaras to be observed. The first was to bring fourth into the world children of noble outlook and character. The third was to create a means for women to be freed from worldly existence. As the Swamiji put it: " A man who is not yet fully mature inwardly is assisted in his karma by his wife. By doing so, by being totally devoted to her husband, she achieves maturity to a degree greater than he does".

Mahatma Gandhi put it in another way. According to him the ideal that marriage aims at is that of spiritual union through the physical. The human love that it incarnates is intended to serve as a stepping stone to divine or universal love. Underfiled love between husband and wife took one nearer to God than any other love. In one of his many essays Gandhi wrote; "The wife is not the husband'd bond slave, but his companion and his help-mate, and an equal partner in all his joys and sorrows... The married state is as much a state of discipline as any other. Life is a duty, a probation. Married life is intended to promote mutual good, both here and hereafter. It is meant to serve humanity."

Unconsciously, Gandhi defined dasoha in marriage. In effect it was service to humanity. Marriage is not just a contact between two people. That would be giving it a poor certificate! Marriage is much more. It is not just taking care of or loving each other either, though that is a necessary ingredient. In marriage one has to seek dasoha, as Poojya Appaji notes" in every thing including begetting children".

This is taking the concept of marriage to fresh heights. Appaji does not minimise the physical aspect of marriage which he considers "beautiful", which indeed it is. But marriage, again, implies "the inter-action of two mids" as much as the "mingling of two bodies". Marriage is a kind of "imprisonment" but an improsonment that is relished, because it brings two souls together in the service of God. In a marriage there is perfect equality. There is no contradiction in a wife looking up to her husband as the Lord and Master considering that the husband in turn has to regard his wife as Mahadevi. This implies that each holds the other in the highest regard so that together they can render true service. In looking up to her husband, the wife no more deans herself than a husband does in treating his wife as goddess.This is true consummation.

XII

Mahadasoha Sutra

Can a devotee of Shiva
Demolish a Shiva Temple ?
Can a devotee of Vishnu
Demolish a Vishnu Temple?
Can a devotee of Jina
And Buddha
Demolish basadhis
And Viharas?
Can Christians
And Mahommadans
Demolish Churches
And Mosques?
Lord,
Demolish they can
The stones that go
To make the Walls
But not You.
There is only
One God for
All religions.
Names you have
Many
But in truth
You are one.
Destruction is
Wrought
Not for love
Of you
But in pursuit
Of man's own
Fanaticism.
Destroy nothing
Tear down nothing.
Abuse not,
Nor cause pain
To others
By your harsh
Words.
The body which is
Greater than
A Temple

Contd...

That is bestowed
By God Himself
Should not be harmed.
The Lord who lives
In that body
Should not be harmed.
To injured such a body
Is more of a sin
Than destroying
The temple of God.
Giving pain to
Pranajangama
That lives in
The body
Is worse than
Destroying the
Image of God
In a temple.
The same of division
Exists
In the minds of Man;
Nowhere else.
If you see yourself
In everything
Around you,
You will know
That differences
Exist only in
Our minds
Not elsewhere.
Even if you are Hurt,
Hurt not others:
Therein lies dasoha.
For the sharanas say:
The reason is
In not giving
And not giving
And not receiving
Others are made happy.
Shedding ill-will,
Seeing God in all Creatures
Desiring only good for all:
That is dasoha.

Sutra -XII

SutraXII embodies all that is beautiful and noble in life's earnest journey.It sums up everything that has been said of yore by Christ in his Sermon on the Mount, by the Buddhain his many sayings, by Mahatama Gandhi and by scores of other savants in precise, life-inspiring words. It even goes beyond the Ten Commandments of Moses. Kill not, hate not, destroy nothing, do not indulge in abuse, do not cause pain to others, see yourself in all living beings. Poojya appaji has stated in his own eloquent way what others have said before him, in different words. Consider this:

Blessed are the meek; for they shall inherit the earth.
Blessed are they which do hunger and thirst after right cousness for they shall be filled.
Blessed are the merciful; for they shall obtain mercy.
Blessed are the pure of heart; for they shall see God
Blessed are the peace-makers; for they shall be called children of God.

St. Mathews

Or

Thou shalt love their neighbour as thyself

Or

Let us not be weary in well-doing: for in due season we shall reap.

Or

Though I have all faith, so that I could move mountains
And have not charity, I am nothing.
And though I bestow all my goods to feed the poor and
Though I give my body to be burnt and have not charity, It profiteth me nothing.

Charity suffereth long, and is kind; charity envieth
Not; charity vaunteth not itself, is not puffed up.
Doth not behave itself unseemly, seeketh not her own, Is not
easily provoked, thinketh no evil.

Here the word charity does not mean giving alms, but means 'Love'. Love, says the Bible never faileth but it endures all things and, in the end, emerges victorious.

Or

take the Dhammapada. The Buddha defines who a true brahmana is.

He who is thoughtful, blameless, settled, dutiful without passions,

and has attained the highest end,him I call in deed a Brahmana.

Him I call indeed a Brahmana who does not offend by body,

Word or thought, and is controlled on these three points.

Him I call a Brahmana who, after cutting all fetters,

Never grembles, is free from bonds and unshackled.

Him I call a Brahama who, though he has committed no offence endures reproach, stripes and bonds.

Him I call a Brahmana who, does not cling to sensual pleasures, like water on a lotus leaf...

Him I call a Brahmana who in this world has risen above both ties, good and evil, who is free from grief, from sin and impurity.

A Brahmana is not one by caste but by the extent of his spiritual growth. The Buddha might just have easily described who is a true dasohi.

To Mahatma Gandhi non-violence-ahimsa-was the ultimate law (paramo dharma). As life he attempted to become a true desohi. He shunned anger, cruelty, killing, ill-will cards others, fanaticism, divisiveness.During different times he said:

I cannot intentionally hurt anything that lives, much less fellow human beings, eventhough they may do the greatest wrong to me and mine.

God is found more often in the lowliest of His creatures than in the high and wighty. I am struggling to reach that status...

My soul refuses to be satisfied so long as it is a helpess witness of a single wrong or a single misery.

We have to make truth and non-violence not matters for mere individual practice but for practice by groups and communities and nations.

The very first step in non-violence is that we cultivate in our daily life as between ourselves, truthfulness, humility tolerance and loving kindness.

Without ahimsa it is not possible to seek and find Truth.

Ahimsa and Truth are so intertwined that it is practically impossible to disentangle and separate them. Ahimsa is the means; Truth is the end.

Violence can only be effectively met by non-violence.

Ahimsa is the highest ideal. It is one of the world's great principles which no power on earth can wipe out.

Poojya Appaji starts by making a general statement. That there is but one Supreme Power, known by many names. It is stated unequivocally in that one line.

Ekam sat; vipra bahudaa vadanti

There is but one Truth though Sages speaks of it in many voices. That one Supreme Power persists and cannot be confined within the walls of a temple, church or mosque. These can be destroyed, but how can one destroy the Power within? One knows God, Supreme Power, by many names; but God is one, whole, Indivisible.

The sense of division, adds Poojya Appaji, is in the mind; it is not so in Reality. In reality, God is one. Further more, if one sees oneself reflected in all things living and existing, in sthavara and jangama, one sees the force unifying all. This is true dasoha.

As Poojya Appaji puts it so beautifully, there is divinity in every human being. Giving pain to pranajangama that lives in the body of that being, then, is worse than destroying the image of God in a temple.

The body is what God has bestowed; harming it is harming the purpose of God. To respect life is to practice dasoha.

XIII
Mahadasoha Sutra

Lingachara
Sadachara
Sivachara
Ganachara
Bhrityachara
These five-fold acts
Are five aspsects
Of dasoha,
My friend.
Awareness of
Nothing else
Other than linga
Is dasoha
And that is
Lingachara.
All activity
Ceaselessly done
In spirit of Dasoha
Is Sadachara.
Seeing Shiva
In all living beings
Is dasoha
And that is
Shivachara.
And to hear not

Contd....

Any insult to Shiva
That too,
Is dasahoa
Which is ganachara.
Considering
Shiva sharanas
As greater than
Shiva himself
And in that knowledge
Offering them
All you possess
In body and mind
Is dasoha
And it is Brithyachara.
Practising
These five acharas
Always in the spirit
Of dasoha
Is the essence of
Dasoha dharma,
My friend.

Sutra - XIII

Just as there are six stages in bhakti on the way to attain perfection, prescribed for the devotee are the five rules of conduct Panchaachaara. These are the wearing of a linga on the body known as lingaachaara, being pure in one's daily activities or sadaachaara, striving hard for the establishment of the Order of Saivism or Shivaacharra, being dutiful and responsible to the team of Saiva devotees or Ganaachaara and finally serving the devotees with humility or Bhrityaachaara.

Together these five rules of conduct constitute the five aspects of dasoha. This sutra merely elaborates on them in simple but easily assimilable terms. The important thing is to be constantly aware of the linga. The linga must illuminate one's consciousness at all times. It must suffuce one's being. Similarly all activity ceaselessly done must be in the spirit of dasoha. Here Poojya appaji has a point to make. According to him while one must serve ceaselessly it should be service without the serve being aware of he is serving. Serving for the sake of Siva or God, says Poojya Appaji is no service at all. The doer should never feel he is doing. The detachment should be total. The Gita, for example, talks about nishkama karma. Doing anything without desiring the fruits thereof. But dasoha goes even beyond that. The doer must not even be aware that he is doing. That is the ultimate perfection.

Poojya Appaji puts it this way: if we do something shedding our ego in the process, that becomes Shivaswaroop. As it is said in Kannada: bayasi bandaddu bhoga, what is done in anticipation of results is bhoga, satisfaction of one's ego. But what is done in a desireless manner bayasade bandaddu is god's gift, linga prasada. In this case there is no distinction between god's wishes and devotee. Thus Meerabai was given poison, but she took it as god's prasad and therefore god's wish. She survived. As Poojya Appaji very rightly states, devotion starts when intellect ceases to be.

Sivachaara, may it be said, is more than merely striving hard for the establishment of Saivism. That would be taking a rather narrow view of the subject. Sivaachaara is seeing Siva in all living things, accepting the fact there is divinity in all life in whatsoever form.

Gana can be loosely defined as a group, a clan, a society, a conglomerate, a fellowship and dasoha implies total loyalty to the gana in one's daily activities. Fellowship implies submission to the larger community, of placing one's personal interests as secondary to the interests of the larger group. Indeed, as Poojya Appaji proceeds to state, the Sivasharanas are greater than Siva himself. To serve them in thought, word and deed is described as brithyachara. And that remains the true essence of dasoha.

When one is the servant of the sarvant of the Lord, one is close to the Lord Himself. It is serve at its most sublime, dasoha, no less.

XIV

Mahadasoha Sutra

What is there
In a mere idol ?
So saying
People prayed
In open space.
But what is there
In open space?
So saying
Some built temples
And set up
Idols within
And worshipped there.
O Lord!
Since you're both
Form and Formless,
With and without
A form.
Formless
Enlightenment
In the form of body
Is worshipped
As jangama.
That formlessness
Installed in form
Is jangama linga
Which accepts worship.
So Basava
And other holy ones
Have said.
The ideal way
To worship is this:
It is
Attaining dasoha by
Seeking God
Through jangama.

Sutra - XIV

Down the ages Man has sought to understand the concept of God and has often, and understandably, seen him, in his own image. How can one define the indefinable, picture the un-illustrable? If God can be recognised in human form he could not be god, surely? It is easy to say that God is every one and everything, that he is Infinite, formless. Sankara has in one of his great invocations to Siva described him in entirely negative terms. Not this, not this. He is sat-chit-ananda. But yet for all the brilliance of Sankara's evocative verse we are still left groping. Sri Krishna tried to show Himself to Arjuna and the warrior is at a loss for words. Arjuna sees the Vishwa Rupa:

Pashyama devamsthava deva dehe
sarvamsthatha bhutavishesha sanghan
brahmanamishamkamalasanastham
Rushinaha sarvanuraganshca divyan

(I see in you all the gods, all living matter, brahma himself, the rishis and represents)

aneka bahudaravakranetram
panhyamitva sarvathonantharupam
nantham namadhyamna punastha vadim
pashyami vishveshwara vishwa yupa.

(I see endless arms,stomachs, faces, eyes; I see the infinite everywhere but I cannot see your beginning, the middle and the end!)

The chapter on Vishwa Rupais an exercise in the sheer futility of knowing Him who is Unknowable.The Lord is VishwaRupa, all that is in creation;Arjuna is dazzled by what he sees:

Divi soorya sahasrasyabhavedyugapaduthitha
Yadi bhasadhrashi sa syadbhasasthasya mahatmana

(The lord is brighter than a thousand suns brighter than if all the suns were together to shine in the splendourous skies).

Arjuna is befuddled. He sees the Lord in all his manifestations. And yet was that all to God? Were Arjuna wise he could have seen God in a grain of sand.

To say that God is indescribable and therefore no attempt should be made to describe him is neither here nor there. The human mind seeks god, wishes to concretise Him who is unconcretisable. But shouldn't we respect the human in us? Poojya Appaji in this sutra brings out beautifully the contradictions within the human mind. Why confine God in a physical form? How can the formless god be transformed into an idol? So there is logic in man saying that he would rather pray in open space, symbolic of the immanance of the creator.

But the mind continues to be baffled. It wants somethings to focus itself on.It wants to imprison the formless into a form. Hence the temples, the icons. Can we blame it in its ceaseless search for the Innfinite?

It requires an exceptionally intuitive mind to understand the Ultimate Reality. The Gita puts this way:

Twewaham jathunaasum
Na tvam nehmehjanadhipaha
No chaiva na bhavishyamah
Sarve vyamathahaparam

(There never was a time when I was not, nor you northese rulers of men, nor will there be ever a time when all of us shall cease to be–Chap 2 verse 12) Or again:

Vaasatho vidhyathe bhaavo
nabhaavoh vidhyatheh sathah
ubhayorapi dhrishontha
stavanayohstaathatva darshibhih

(The unrealhas no being; the realneverceases tobe; the final truth about themboth has thusbeen perceived by the seers of Ultimate Reality) well said. But human dilemma remains.

Theheart seeks what the mind knowscannotberealised. Sowhere dowego fromhere?

Here Poojya Appaji gives the seekersomesolace. Formless enlightnment in the form of bod, he consoles, is worshippedas jangama. That formlessness installed in form is *jangama linga,* which accepts worship.

The mind is at rest.

XV

Mahadasoha Sutra

There are many
Who insist
That re-birth is
Inevitable.
There are equally
Many who insist
That there isn't
Anything like it.
Many again say
That birth and death
Are what mark
A wordly man.
But Lord Basava said:
Our sharanas
Have niether birth nor death.
He also said:
If I take birth,
I'll lead a blessed life
Serving guru-linga-jangama
Receiving teertha
And prasad.
As had been said:
Does it matter
Whether a sandalwood tree
Grows in a jungle
Or in a town?
Either way
Its fragrance
Stays the same.
When Shiva
Takes form on earth
It is as a dasohi.
When he has to
Depart,
It is back to
Himself.
So his devotee
In life is
Immersed in

Contd...

The linga
On his death
He returns again
To the linga,
Here in action
On earth
He is Uma's Consort
The action
Over
He is Swayambhu
Self-born.
Thus wise,
In the illustrious
House,
Where a sharana
Does his dasoha
Holier it is than
A Temple to Shiva
Himself.
Wherefore
The journey to
That House
Become a
Pilgrimage
And sighting
A sharana
Becomes a
Vision
And receiving
What is given
Becomes
Prasad itself.
Conquering the
Chain of Birth
And death,
That is the
Essence of
Dasoha,
My friend.

Sutra - XV

Lord Basava once said: "Our Sharanas have neither birth nor death". It is a statement pregnant with meaning. If there is neither birth nor death what is? Does it mean there is, infact, no such thing as existence? It is an intriguing thought. The answer should be self-evident. There exists the linga, the highest godhead, the Transcendant Truth the Final Reality, or the Parabrahma. Nothing can change that. That truth can take form, as Poojya Appaji states, if Shiva comes to earth. But how does one recognise such a Shiva? Why, when one meets the dasohi in whom perfection is instituted. So, when the perfect dasohi departs the returns to what he always was: the Linga. Where then is life, where death? In the beginning was the Linga; and in the end all that remains is still the Linga. One can't take away anything from what is: the Ultimate Reality. It is stated very eloquent terms by the Shantipatha:

Poornamadhaa poornamidham
Poornathpoornamudhachyathe
Poornasya poornamadhaya
Poornamevavashishyate

(That is complete; this is complete; The complete cannot be diminished for whatever emerges from it still leaves the ultimate Reality complete).

Once does not, therefore, argue whether there is re-birth; what prevails is continuity. In continuity there is no break; as Poojya Appaji states, when Shiva takes form on earth he comes as a dasohi. He comes as Uma's consort. This should not be taken in the literal sense. Uma and Shiva are the two-fold personification of brahman. The primeval substance. Sc when we speak of Shiva and Uma, we speak about the unity of two attributes: those of Shiva: self-existence, essential purity, intruitive wisdom, infinite intelligence, freedom from all bonds, infinite grace or love, omnipotence and infinite blisss and those of Uma: eternal knowledge, limitless space, splendorous light and tranquillity.

When we see the confluence of the two forces on earth, especially in a Sharana we know there Shiva exists. Where a Sharana lives and is immersed in dasoha where is there need for a temple? The Sharana's residence is holier than a temple and a journey to that residence becomes a pilgrimage and what the Sharana gives becomes prasad itself.

A journey to the home of the Sharana is a journey to self-understanding. Let this be remembered: Shiva is the only reality, the one without a second: Ekamevadwitiya. He is infinite consciousness and absolute independence. He is the foundation of all knowledge. As has been well stated, he makes the world appear in Himself as if it were distinct from himself, though not really so " By his wonderful power (shakti) inherent in him, God appears in form. The changing manifestations of Shiva do not stain his purity and unchanging nature since. He transcends his own manifestations. The effort to understand this in effect is what the journey to the Sharana is all about. The understanding is thirth, the acceptance is prasad.

So when Basava says that if he takes birth he can only serve guru-linga-jangama he speaks of the ultimate aim of all mankind: to understand the meaning of existence by the supreme act of dasoha.

And when the understanding finally dawns both birth and death fall in place as part of that continuity that is eternal. Thereby one conquers the chain of birth and death, seeing in them Shiva's eternal play-and ploy. There is no death: there is only return to the linga., ever-existing, ever present, whole, unchangeable, formless, Sharana of such attributes as birth and death, for how can what exists eternally have such attributes, as birth and death? Shiva is swayambhu,·self-born.

XVI
Mahadasoha Sutra

What is the difference
Between worldly
And otherworldly
Concerns,
My friend?
What is meant by
Sharana wife
And linga husband ?
The bond with a wife
Is love.
The bond with children
Is belonging.
The bond with kinsfolk
Is friendship.
When the bond with
Teachers, elders, God,
Is made fully worthy
Of Trust,
It is transformed
Into the dasoha
Of Bhakti
When the Bhakta's devotion
To dasoha
Is unwavering
The bhakta becomes
Maheshwara.
When Maheshwara's
Unwavering devotion

Contd...

To dasoha
Gets focussed,
He is prasadi.
When the prasadi's
Devotion to dasoha
Gets enlightened
He is pranalingi.
When pranalingi's
Devotion to dasoha
Combines with
Divine bliss,
Then he is Sharana.
When that sharana's
Spouses' devotion
To dasoha
Fuses with linga
Husband,
Then he is aikya.
Since the doer
And the activator
Are the same;
Since all
Practice is
Endowed with
Dasoha bhakti
Know then
That this is
Shatsthala dasoha.

Sutra - XVI

Sutra 16 is unquestionably one of the most profound written by Poojya Appaji and describes the various stages by which one may attain unity with the godhead. He calls it aikya-unity, total integration.

The road to unity with the godhead-the ultimate Reality-is an arduous one and is not to be achieved overnight. As in any great effort-like reaching the summit of Mount Everest-one proceeds step by step, each step taking one higher and higher until the height is reached. How is aikya achieved?

One can start with one of the great saying in Sanskrit literature:

satsangatva nissangatvam
nissangatve nirmohatmam
nirmohatve nischalachittam
nischalachittae mokshamprapti.

The wise assert that to attain moksha, the final liberation, one must start with satsang, the cultivation of good company. One must choose one's friends carefully. They must be persons of impeccable goodness, men attuned to god. That is the first step. In such company the individual grows steadily in spiritual development to the point that he can do away with all company: nissangha. When one has attained that stage he reaches the next one, that of detachment. The Gita says:

Jitamanah prasaantsaya
Pramaatmaa samaahitah
Shi to shnasukhadukheshu
Tatha maanapamaanoyoh

(To him who has subdued his senses and whose mind is thoroughly unpertubed and calm God becomes manifest).

When the mind is free of detachment, it is possible to attain the next stage, that of nischalachitta-stead fastness of the mind when the mind can concentrate wholly and solely on the Ultimate Reality. The last and inevitable stage from steadfastness of the mind to attainment of moksha-liberation-comes naturally.

Therefore, says the Gita:

Yogi Yunjita satatam
aatmaanam rahasi sthitah
ekaaki yatachittaatmaa
nirashiraparigraha

(Let the yogi apply his mind to meditation constantly staying in a secured place with his mind and body under restraint, having eschewed desires and receiving no favours from other).

If this is understood it is easy to understand what Poojya Appaji speaks about attaining aikya. He starts with the simple question: "What is meant by Sharana wife and linga husband"? The answer comes through beautifully. The bond with a wife is love. The bond with children is belonging. The children belong to the couple. Then there is the bond with kinsfolk. Now this is neither love, nor belonging but friendship. When the bond with teachers, elders and God is made fully worthy of Trust that is transformed into the dasoha of bhakti-service through devotion. When that devotional service becomes unwavering, the bhakta now gets transformed into Maheshwara and when Maheshwara's own devotion to dasoha gets focused he gets Prasad-the grace of God.

Next comes the prasadi's own devotion to dasoha when he gets enlightenment and becomes praanalingi-Ultimate Reality gets a life of its own. From this with further devotion to dasoha and divine bliss we get the Sharana.

Sharana, writes Poojya Appaji at the very start, can be compared to the wife in a wife/husband relation where the husband is linga. When Sharana and linga are fused, is reached the ultimate stage-aikya. So here are the steps the shatshthala dasoha. The bond of Trust get transformed into the dasoha of bhakti.

Bhaktha + unwavering dasoha = Maheshwara.
Maheshwara + unwavering devotion= prasadi.
Prasadi + enlightened dasoha = Praanalingi
Pranalingi + dasoha + divine bliss = Sharana.
Sharana + linga = aikya.

When aikya is achieved, what else is there to aspire for?

The same thoughts are expressed in a different way in the Gita:

mayyeva mana aadhatsva
mayi buddhim niveshaya
nivashishyasi mayyeva
ata oordhwam na shamsaya

(Fix your mind on me, alone, let your thoughts abide in Me; thereafter you will live in me, i.e. attain the state of perfect bliss and there is no doubt about it.)

And isn't that aikya?

XVII

Mahadasoha Sutra

I tried talking
To you.
It was like a
Dumb man
Expressing himself
Through band-sings.
My sound sings
Could have been
The sounding
Of a conch.
Attempting to
Talk to you,
I stood as if dumb.
Listening to me,
Was it like
An elder being
Annoyed
At the sound of
Children banging
On the drums ?
Language is
But a vehicle;
It is not God.
The one Language
To speak with God
Is bhakit dasoha,
God's only tongue.
Be jyotirlinga
Through wordless Talk.
That is the way
Of Mahadasoha
Which sees
Without eyes
Like the Three-Eyed One.

Sutra - XVII

This must be the most beautiful of all the nineteen sutras written by Poojya Appaji. It is a description of the sense of happy helplessness the devotee feels in addressing himself to God-the ultimate Reality. The devotee-let us imagine him standing in front of God-wants so desperately to address him, but is dumstruck. Words fail him. He wants to convey his wishes but he is overawed. He want to express his happiness but just does not know how to. He stands there trying to speak but words do not come through. He clears his throat but feels like a dumb man trying to express himself through hand-signs. It is not that God has just revealed himself to his devotee as Krishna revealed himself to Arjuna. When Krishna revealed his *Vishwa roopa* Arjuna was understandably stunned. This *Vishwa roopa* was something new to him. Arjuna had seen nothing like that before. There he stands, not knowing what to do. At this point the Gita is eloquent. The Vishwa roopa-brighter than a thousand suns-dazzles Arjuna. But what this devotee is facing is not the terrifying form, but the benevolent God who completely captivates him. It is not fear that strikes him dumb, but the sheer joy of meeting the Lord. The Lord does not always have to look frightening. In the *Brahma sutra* (5.39) it is stated: *ramaadhi murtishu kalaa niyamena tishthan*. The Lord is eternally situated in hundreds and thousands of forms. Here the devotee is standing in front of the Lord wishing to communicate. But love, awe, devotion, fulfillment overwhelm him. He wonders: am I behaving like a child banging on the drums to attract the attention of his elders? Is that right? Is he being childish? The devotee is overpowered by the presence. He is happy, pleased and yes, confused as well. He is delightfully unsure of what to say or do. Disarmingly he says to God. "I am trying to talk to you, God but I can't! Help me!"

It is the frustration of the lover in front of his Beloved: wishing to talk, wishing to under burden himself but love over-powers him. He can only stand there, mute. Some of these feelings are expressed by the saint-poet Purandara Dasa in some of the most beautiful lines:

Ninna nodi danyanadhene
He Srinivasa
ninna nodi dhanyanadheno

(Oh Lord, Srinivasa, looking at you I am fulfilled) or when he says, addressing the Lord:

naa ninnol anya beduvudilla
yenna hridaya kamaladelu
nindiru Hariye

(O Lord, there is nothing more that I will ask except that you stay within my heart).

This is devotion-bhakti-at its purest. And this is the single thread that is common to the lives of all saints, Nivritti, Jnandev, Sopana, Muktabai, Eknath, Namdeo Tukaram, the thread of pure devotion. It calls for no intellectual gymnastics. It makes no demand on one's body as would asceticism, with its praying and fasting. Teresa of Avila, the Christian saint would have understood it as Francis of Assisi or Ramakrishna paramahansa of Belur. Kanakadasa sang of it. When devotion fills the heart, the tongue is silent. There is only one possible language in which to coverse with the supreme: it is the *bhakti dasoha*, the total surrender to God. Language has its limitations. Language is not god. But bhakti dasoha is limitless, it is language that the Lord understands. It is His language. Poojya Appaji "Bejyotirlinga, through wordless talk, that is the way to mahadasoha". This is a wholly stainable *sadhana. Rabindranath Tagore* has dealt with it in his book with the same title.

When *bhakti dasoha* begins, words end. But one speaks now in the language of the Gods.Communication is instant. There is perfect harmony between the *bhakti*-the devotee and the supreme God head.The ancient rishis knew that only too well.

Samprapyainam rishayejnanatriptah
kritamano vitargah prashantah
te sarvagamsarvatah prapya dhirah
yuktamanahsarvametavishanti

(They who have attained the supreme soul in knowledge were filled with wisdom and having found him in union with the soul were in perfect harmony with the inner self; they having realised him in the heart were free from all selfish desires and having experienced him in all activities of the world, had attained calmness. The rishis were they who having reached the supreme God from all sides had found abiding peace, had become united with all, had entered into the life of the universe).

All activities of the world are surrendered to Him in *bhakti dasoha;* the self gets dissolved. There is only Jyotirlinga.And then *aikya.*

XVIII

Mahadasoha Sutra

Frightened was I
Like a man
Chased by a dog
When I thought
This body is mine.
Frightened was I
Like one faced
By a lion
When I through
This mind is mine.
As I considered
Myself, imprisoned
In my thoughts,
The darkness deepened
My terror of death
Appeared as a ghost
To torment me.
But before the dog
And the lion
And the ghost
That is death
Could touch me,
I offered my body
To Ishtalinga,
My mind
To Pranalinga
And my thinking
To Bhavalinga.
Whereupon
When I felt
Chased by a dog,
I felt the presence
Of the lion,
And lost the fear
Of the dog.
Even so,
When I felt chased
By a lion,

Contd.....

I felt the presence
Of the ghost,
And lost the fear
Of the lion !
And were the ghost
That is death
To chase-me
In the darkness,
In the light of
Bhakti dasoha
Death would die
And darkness
Lie exposed
Naked to the eye.
When Death dies
It becomes
The Great Door
To God,
Mahanavami, no less.
Living this
Fierce bhakti,
I became
Shiva Himself.
And, like a plant,
A tree, a vine
That bring forth
In turn,
First flower,
Then fruit,
Even so
Life should ripen,
End
In Truth, Beauty
And Bliss.
That is
Dasoha's Way,
Says,
Mahadasohi
Sharana Basava.

Sutra - XVIII

To understand this remarkable sutra, one must go back to the Gita-chapter 13-in which the nature of the body, mind and death is discussed in full.

The body, mind and death stand for certain values which Poojya Appaji discusses in metaphorical terms.

What is metaphor? It is simply a figure of speech in which a term or phrase is applied to something to which it is not literally applicable, in order to suggest a resemblance, as in a mighty fortress is our God. In this sutra, Poojya Appaji speaks about a dog, a lion and the terror of death, but if one substitutes the words with *prakriti, purusha* and *kshetra* one can understand what he is trying to explain. In chapter 13 Arjuna asks Krishna:

> Prakritim purusham Chaiva
> kshetram kshetra-jnam eva cha
> etad-veditum ichchami
> jnaanam jhhneyam ca keshava

(O Krishna, I wish to know about *prakriti* (nature), *purusha* (the enjoyer) and the field and the knower of the field and of knowledge and the object of knowledge).

Then follows a brilliant exposition of the three. Krishna tells Arjuna that the body is called the field and that one who knows this body is called the knower of the field. The conditioned soul is entrapped in material existence and he attempts to lord it over material nature. And so, according to his capacity to dominate material nature, he gets a field of activity. The field of activity is the body. And what is the body? The body is made of senses. Krishna says:

> mahaabhutaani ahankaare
> buddhir avyaktam eva cha

indriyaani dashaikam cha
pancha chendriyagocharaah

(The five great elements, *ahankara*(ego), *buddhi* (intelligence) and also *avyakta* (unmanifest *prakriti*) the five objects of senses, the eleven organs (five of senses and five of action and mind)-all these are called *kshetra*).

The person who identifies himself with the body is called the *kshetrajna*, the knower of the field. There is a difference between the field and the knower of the field. The body consists of the senses. The supreme Lord is Hrishikesha-the controller of the senses. As one scholar has put it: "He is the original controller of the senses, just as the king is the original controller of all the activities of the State; the citizens are secondary controllers". The Lord says: "I am also the knower". He is actually the supreme knower. For a man to think that the body is his, in the circumstances is *a jnana*. Similarly for a man to think that the mind is his is also *a jnana*. Even to think that in the end it is he who dies, is also yet another example of *a jnana*. What, in the end, exists? Not the body, not the mind, not death. It is the Ultimate, defined by Poojya Appaji in terms of the Ishtalinga, Pranalinga and Bhavalinga.

Says Bhaktivedanata Swami Prabhupada: "One has to understand the position of *prakriti* (nature), *purusha* (the enjoyer of nature) and *Iswara* (the knower who dominates or controls nature and the individual soul). One should not confuse the three in their different capacities. This material world is nature; it is the field of activities; the enjoyer of nature is the living and above them both is the supreme controller, the Personality or Godhead. It is stated in *Svetasavara Upanishad*:

Bhoktaa bhogyam preritaaram cha matvaa
Sarvam proktam tri-vidham Brahman etat,

(There are three Brahman conceptions: prakriti is Brahman as the field of activities, and the jiva is also brahman and is trying to control material nature and the controller of both of them is also Brahman, but he is the factual controller".

But Poojya Appaji see things differently. Beyond the body and the mind and death he sees the spirit of bhakti dasoha, the Great Liberator.

Bhakti dasoha frees man from his foolish belief that the body is his or that the mind is his or that he is due to perish. When man surrenders his body to Ishtalinga, his mind to Pranalinga and his thinking to Bhavalinga what, then, is there to be afraid of? Man goes beyond the beyond to the ultimate, Shiva himself.

It is a valid and brilliant concept. He who understands it understands all. As the Gita itself says:

> Ya evam vetti purusham
> Prakrtim ca gunaih saha
> Sarvathaa vartamaano'pi
> Na sa bhuyo 'bhijaayate

(One who understands this philosophy concerning nature, the living entity and the interaction of the modes of nature is sure to attain salvation. He will not take birth here again, regardless of his present position).

And that Dasoha's Way.

XIX
Mahadasoha Sutra

To understand
The ways of God
One must
Follow the guru.
To understand
Kudala sanga
One must be
Among the sharanas.
Holier than
Deva Loka
The Abode of Gods,
Is the home of
The Shiva bhakta.
Holier than Varanasi
Is the courtyard
Of the Shiva bhakta.
Holier than
Mount Kailas,
Is the body of
The Shiva bhakta Wherefore
The wise ones say:
Forbidden
Is earthly pilgrimage.
True pilgrimage
According to them
Is the pilgrimage
To the sharanas.
That is sadachara
That seeks
Companionship
Of Shiva's bhaktas,
Even if one
Has to travel
A hundred thousand miles
To be with them.
And with them,
If you serve,
Yours is God,
So say the wise.
Fellowship
With the sharanas, then,
Truly is The essence
of dasoha.

Sutra - XIX

There is the ancient story of Shiva and his two sons, Ganesh and Kartikeya and how Siva tested them. As we all know the *vahana* of Ganesh is a rat and of Kartikeya, the peacock. One day Siva summoned both his sons and promised an award to first who went round the world ten times, and became a winner. Kartikeya was at first a little diffident. How could Ganesh ever make it when all that he had for a vehicle was a rat? Mounting his peacock, Kartikeya could make the rounds in no time and he did not want to be unfair to his brother. But Ganesh had no such fears. He was willing to join the race. Nothing would dissuade him from entering it even when he was pointedly told of his handicap.

So the race bagam. One can imagine Siva saying: Ready? All set? Go! And off kartikeya went without bothering for a moment to look behind. If he did he might have wondered at his brother Ganesh who was contendedly standing by idly, not moving an inch, "what?" asked Siva, though he must have known the answer, "aren't you participating in the race?". "Of course, I am" came Ganesh's reply, "you just watch and see!"

Kartikeya, sure of winning was in great spirits as his peacock flew round the world with lightning speed. Round One, Round Two, Round Three, Round Four, Round Five... but as kartikeya was in and out of sight, Ganesh still stood by Siva's side, unmoving. The *Ganesh* watched Ganesh in wonder. Had he conceded defeat even before the race had begum? Round Six, Seven, Eight, Nine... and still Ganesh seemed lethargic. But just as everyone had given up hope, Ganesh mounted his rat leisurely went round Siva, once, twice, thrice, four times, five times... ten times even while Kartikeay was sweating it out his last round and then, standing in front of Siva asked for the award.

Siva smiled.

"Lord" said Ganesh, "you are the world, indeed, the creator of the entire Universe! What foolishness is it to fly around when all I have to do is to do your pradakshina ten times!"

And he won the prize.

And that is the point that Poojya Appaji makes in his last Sutra. Where Siva bhaktas (devotees of Siva) are there dwellas Siva. Ergo, the home of the Siva *bhakta* is holier than *Deva Loka* and persona of the *bhakta* surely is holier than Mount Kailas?

What necessity, then, is to go on pilgrimage when the holiest of holy places may be next door in the home of the *Sharana? Go,* says Poojya Appaji, and seek the companionship of the Sharana, even if he should be hundred thousand miles away. For where the Sharana is, there God dwells. And fellowship with the *Sharanas* is the essence of *dasoha*.

The sutra has an invaluable moral. One doesn't have to make pilgrimages to distance places in search of God. God does not dwell only in far away pilgrim centers. In the Bible it is said: The kingdom of God is within you!

We flee from God;we look for him everywhere except where we should really look for him: in the home of the Sharana!

Indeed, even in one's own heart!

English poet Francis Thompson makes a similar point in his poem. *The Hound of Heaven*.There is this man who is fleeing from life.

"down the right and down the days,down the arches of the years, down the labyrinthine ways of his own mind", but to no effect. Finally, tired, weary, he stops. The poet new says:

"Halt by me that footfall:
Is my gloom, after all
Shade of His hand, outstretched caressingly?

"Ah,fondest, blindest,weakest,
I am He whom thou seekest!
Thou dravest love from thee, who dravest Me!"

And then there is the story of kim who accompanies a monk in his eternal search for the beginning of the river of Life. Miles and miles they walk, untried eager, determined but they see no end for their search.

Then one day the monk stops, at a place it seemedno where from no where. But there is a glod on his face.To his surprised disciplehe tells: Our journey now is ended. Here at my feet is the beginning. We need fare no more!

There is no need to go seaching for Siva.Siva is there wherever one serves with the *Sharanas*.

In that fellowship is *dasoha*.
And that said, everthing is said.

XX

Mahadasoha Sutra

That, O friend, in Kayaka?
That which is done without ego
That which is done with devotion
That which is done with
Total concentration of mind
That is Kayaka.
And what is dasoha?
That which is given without ego
That which is given with devotion
That which is given with
Single-mindedness
That is dasoha.
And what is prasada?
That which is received with devotion
That which is received in tranquility
That is prasada.
Whatever is done
In total devotion
Without pride
Without ego
Becomes Kayaka.
Becomes worship.
Any devotion
Accompanied with pride
Leads to Karma.
Not even worship
Can truly prevent it.
If what you earn
Is given for the happiness
Of all living beings
With total devotion
Then it is due dasoha.
Such a one
Attains salvation
Remember,
The lord descends on earth
As linga being static

Contd...

As jangama
through movement,
As guru in bestowing
Enlightenment,
It is this trinity
Of Guru-linga-Jangama
That is one
Without a second.
Follow then,
The five-fold conduct:
Be pure in your daily activities
Wear the linga on your body,
Strive for the establishment
Of saivism in your surroundings
Be dutiful to your colleagues
In this enterprise
And serve all devotees
With humility
Thereby
Through the smearing
Of ashes
Through wearing
The sacred rudrakshi chain
And through
The chanting of
Right mantras
One attains dasoha
That, friend,
Is the essence of dasoha.
This also is Tree
And the devotee who
Understands this
Truth
And worships
Without ego
Strives without attachment
Offers without attachment
And received without
Attachment
Acquires prasada
Such a one
Indeed is linga
The presence of God

Sutra - XX

Again and again the question arises: what is kayaka, lbours? Or rather, the question should be, what is true kayaka, labour?

We have the answer in the Gita, in the Upanishads, in Bibble, in fact in every great work where it is said that one strives, not for one's own sake, not in search of wealth, power or for self-aggrandisment but for its own sake. Because work, indeed, is worship.

T.S. Eliot has stated that beautifully in his poem The Rock. The lot of men is ceaseless labour Or ceaseless idleness, which is still harder, Or irrengular labour, which is not pleasant. I have trodden the winepress alone, and I know That it is hard to be really useful, resigning The things that men count for happiness, seeking The goods deeds that lead to obscurity, accepting With equal face those that bring ignominy, The applause of all or the love of none. All men are ready to invest their money But most expect dividends.

I say to you: Make perfect your will I say: Take no thoughtof theharvest But only of proper sowing.

It is a powerful poem.It is said that Eliot was greatly influenced by the Gita when he was young, barely 23.That influence is seen in his several works including. The Waste Land. In the poem quoted above we see that influence at its most profound. He says: "Make perfect your will; take no thought of the harvest, but only of proper sowing."

"Make perfect your will. That is *dasoha*. In perfection lies personal surrender. Perfection does not permit selfness. Indeed, It projects it. Take no thought of the harvest. That is anotherway of saying:*karmanyevadhikarasthe ma paleshu kadachina.*

Do your duty without seeking the fruits there of. Think only of proper sowing. Which is to say, just to your duty. It is your duty to sow. The harvest will take care of itself.

Let us go back to Eliot for a while:
We thank Thee who has moved us to building
To finding, to forming at the ends of our
Fingers and beams of our eyes.
And when we have built an altar to the invisible
Light, we may set thereon the little lights for
Which our hodily Vision is made.
And we thank Thee that darkness reminds us of light
O Light Invisible, we give thanks for Thy great glory!

The poet is thanking God for everything; that is *dasoha* and Eliot is expressing it in his own thought and language. Everything that we have, that which moves us to build, towork with our fingers, with our senses, comes from him, the Almightly. Surrender, say eliot to him who reminds us that darkness only leads to light! It is this that Poojya Appa states with similar felicity in his sutra.That which is done, that which is given, that which is received, all, he says, should be given in utter detachment, sans ego, thought for oneself.That is dasoha.

Thereby
Through the smearing
Of ashes
Through wearing
The sacred rudrakshi
Chain

And through
The chanting of
Right *mantras*
One attains *dasoha*

That, friend
Is the essence of *dasoha*.
This alone is
True
And the devotee who

Understands this
Truth
And worship
Without ego
Strives without attachment,
Offers without attachment
And received without
Attachment
Acquires prasada
The gift of God

Such a one
Indeed in *linga*
The awesome presence of God.

XXI
Mahadasoha Sutra

Uniting body with God
Through the nine-fold path
Is the essence of dasoha.
Thus wise flesh is
Transformed into Mantra,
The invocation to God
Becoming the Gift of God.
Despise not
What is bestowed
To the body:
So has said Basava.
Remember:
No saint has forbidden
Sexual pleasure as such.
For from pleasure
Truth can be realised.
Even as from sour butter
Ghee can be realised
And from food
Strength can be realised.
It is in offering
Everything to God
In the highest
Can the cleansing
Of body and mind
Be realised.
And what, pray,
Is Prasada, Transquillity
The Gift of God?
Serving God

Condt....

Through the objects of
Sanctified smell,
Sanctified taste,
Sanctified touch,
Sanctified sight,
Sanctified sound
All contentment
Sanctified
Because it is dedicated
To God
Becomes prasada
The gift of God.
Wherefore,
Surrender
Everything
That is yours
In heart, mind and wealth
Fully and totally,
In the service of the Lord
Without reserve,
In the service of the Lord
Without reserve,
In full detachment
With he claim that
Anything is yours
Thuswise, attain
Dasaha
Says Mahadashi Sharanabasava.

Sutra - XXI

We now come to the last Sutra. Poojya Appaji says: be one with God through the nine-fold path. Despise not the flesh for why did God give it to us if it was not to be used? What is relevant is not the use but the rightful purpose of that use. The sense are not be be blamed or despised. They have to be dedicated to God "even as from sour butter ghee is realised and from food strength is realised". In his book *The Greatest Thing In The World*, the English philosopher Henry Drummond wirtes:

"The end of life is to do God's will. Now that is a great and surprising revelation.No man ever found that our. It has been before the world (for two thousand years) yet few have found it out. One man will tell you of life is.to be true. Another will tell you it is to deny self. Another will say it is to keep the Ten Commandments. A fourth will point you to the Beatitudes. One will tell you it is to do good. Another that it is to get good, another that it is to be good. But the end of life is none of these things. It is more than all and it includes them all. It is not to get good nor be good nor even to do good it is just what God wills, whether that he be working or waiting, or winning or losing or suffering or recovering, or living or dying. Like little children we must sit at his feet and learn." That is exactly what Poojya Appaji says in his sutra: "Surrender everything that is yours in heart, mind and wealth without reserve".

That is what another philosopher the sufi saint Sai Ro chaldas Sahib says: "Surrender means loss of ego or individual identity. When a seeker comes to his satguru and bows to him, he is supposed to have surrendered to him totally. He must faithfully follow the instructions of his sat guru and bid godbye for ever to his intelligence and cleverness. That marks surrender. A jiva can be stable in surrender when he becomes humble and serves everyone with sincerity and humility. All his actions must he created to his satguru. Thus ego will not arise in him. A seeker should realise that nothing would remain with him after he has surrendered only he who has totally surrendered himself to the Lord and is firm in self surrender can accept His will happily".

Thus is dasoha defined by other philosophers and saints and they speak in different voices but on the same theme.

In effect one has to remember that it is He who gives and he who takes and that every thing is his.

> Mayyeva sakalam jatam mayisarvam pratisthitam
> Mayi sarvam layam yati tad Brahmadvayamasmyaham

Everythingis born out of Me,everything is maintained in Me; Everything merges in Me. I am that Brahma, one without a second).

In such a case,where is the place for Ego?

In the endone can only quote Rabindranath Tagore who expresses dasoha in his own inimitable way in Gitanjali.

> In one salutation to thee, my God let all my senses spread out and touch this world at thy feet.
>
> Like a rain-cloud of July hung low with its burden of unshed showers, let all my mind bend down at they door in one salutation to thee.
>
> Let all my songs gather together their diverse strains into a single current and flow to a sea of silencein one salutation to thee.
>
> Like a flock of homesick cranes flying night and day back to the mountain nests, let all my life take its voyage to its eternal home in one salutation to thee

Salutions, salutations, then to *linga* who appears on earthas *sthavara* and *jangama* and *guru* from him who in *dasoha* surrenders himself to the One, the Only and the Perfect.

Shanti, Shanti, Shanti..

Notes to the Dasoha Sutras

By
Dr. L. Basavaraju

1

1 *DASOHA*: Selfless service to God, to (Guru) the religious teacher and to the Jangama (both in the sense of a holy wanderer and all the living beings, according to Basava.

2 *BASAVA*: an enlightened man who led a socio-religious movement in Karnataka in 12th century.

3 *VACANA*: a form of literary composition, like free verse, in Kannada, a prose poem employed for the spread of saivism in Karnataka by Basava and his followers down to the present day. This vacana type of composition was in vogue prior to Basava and was used by the saiva saints to express mytical experiences.

4 *ISOPANISHAD*: an Upanishad, so called from its beginning Isa; also called Isavasya. It is one of the ten principal Upanishads.

5 *MAHADASOHI S ARANA BASAVA*: authors of vacana literature have their own mark or sign of authorship for their compositions, usually occurring at the end of each composition. The present author of Mahadasoha Sutra also has his mark of authorship as Mahadasohi Sarana Basava at the end of all the sixteen vacanas. "Mahadasohi Sarana Basava" means Sarana Basava, the great servant of God and humanity. Sarana Basava was the Guru of PUJYA SRI DODDAPPA APPA, the first holy man in the line of Sri Sarana Basaveswara Samsthan of Gulbarga.

2

1 *GURU*: a spiritual teacher who initiates the desciple into the religious order, giving him proper instruction,

2 *PRANA*: the breath of life, life that resides in the body.
BHAKTA: a devotee.

3 JANGAMA: a saiva sanyasin, "the God moving about"; anything living and moving about.

4 SERVICE WITHOUT EGO: a phrase used equivalent to dasoha. See 1-1.

5 *LORD OF MEETING RIVERS KUDALA SANGAMA DEVA* literally "Lord Siva that resides at the confluence of two rivers. BASAVA lived at the place, still called Kudalasangama (Bijapur district, Karnataka), and he invokes Kudala Sangamadeva–Lord of the meeting rivers at the end of each of his vacanas.

6 *SIRIYALA-CANGALE*: husband (Siriyala) and wife (Cangale) staunch Saiva devotees, who lived in the time prior to Basava. The story is: Lord Siva appeared to them as a mendicant and insisted that he be served with the flesh of their only son. The devoted couple did so and Lord Siva was so pleased that he made dead child come alive.

7 *SARANA BASAVA*: a saiva saint of 18th century established a religious center in Gulbarga in the house of his desciple Pujya Sri Doddappa Appa, which has since become the center of a socio-religious activity; now called Sri Sarana Basaveswara Samsthan. First head of this illustrious institution was Sarana Basava referred to above and after him came Doddappa Appa his disciple. Currently, Pujya Sri Sharana Basavappa Appa, the eighth in the lineage, heads the institutions.

8 *NIRVANA*: The light of life becoming united with thelight of the Supreme Being; Salvation or Mukti. Nirvana is personified as one's beloved with whom one becomes united after one attains salvation.

9 *KAYAKA*: any labour manual or mental. The fruit of such labour becomes pure and a worthy offering to GURU (teacher), Linga (God) and Jangama (holy mendicant, or any living being) only when it is earned in the honesty of labour.

10 *SENSE OF SELF*: a sense of ego or pride, a sense of self-esteem.

11 *PRASADA*: (1) calmness tranquility, absent of excitement, serenity of disposition, (2) gift of food by the trinity: GURU-LINGA-JANGAMA. (3) The food presented to the Trinity. (4) The remnants of food lift by the Trinity.

3

1 *JANGAMA*: a saiva saint.

2 *JANGAMA LINGA*: God the moving force,

4

1 *MANTRA*: a sacred formula addressed to any individual deity (e.g.OM SIVAYA NAMAH). The primary mantras are said to be 70 million in number and the secondary ones innumerable.

2 *LAKSHMI*: Success, happiness, wealth, riches, heauty; indentified with LAKSHMI and regarded as the wife of Vishnu or Narayana.

5

1 *KARMA*: any work undertaken expecting returns will result in misery, not salvations. So work done with a sense of service is esteemed very high. In vacana literature Karma means sin or sinful action too.

2 *LILA*: mirthful play. The whole creation is thought to be a mirthful play of God Siva. It is said when God in a playful mood, the universe is created, and when that play of Siva is over the involution of the universe takes place–that is the creation loses its name (NAME) and form (RUPA) and everything comes to a stand still.

3 *LINGA*: (1) image of Siva worn on the body or installed in a temple, (2) God Siva,

4 *GURU-LINGA-JANGAMA*: the Trinity: teacher-god-godly man. A devotee worth the name is expected to serve guru (teacher). Worship linga (god), dedicate everything he possesses to Jangama (the god that moves).

5 *Sadhana*: Practice.

6 *BHAKTA*: a devotee of God.

7 *PANCACARA*: Five rules of conduct prescribed for a devotee in saivism.

7

1 *ANGA-LINGA*: ANGA the individual soul, LINGA the universal soul, the God,

2 *BODY OF FLESH AND BODY OF MANTRA*: when the religious teacher (GURU) initiates the desciple into the religious system, the body of flesh of the desciple becomes the body of mantra (body divine) on listening to the guru's chanting of the mantra.

3 *WITH SOMETHING SOUR YOU CAN MAKE SWEET GHEE*: Churning curd, which is sour, butter is made and by heating butter sweet ghee is obtained.

4 *SIX-FOLD LINGA*: The initiate has to progress in Saiva religion through these six stage (1) acara linga (cultivation of good conduct), (2) guru linga (approaching the guru), (3) shiva linga (getting the image of Siva from the guru in order to meditate upon), (4) Jangama linga (serving the Jangama, the highest in the trinity), (5) Prasada linga (obtaining serenity of disposition), (6) Mahalinga (becoming fit to be united with God).

5 *ISHTA-PRANA-BHAVA LINGAS*: Initiating the desciple into religion, the Guru establishes ishta linga on the gross body, prana linga on the inner body and bhava linga on the innermost body of the descriple. The desciple is expected to offer these three lingas respectively his body, his mind and all his possessions by way of worship to God and service to humanity.

6 *BODY DEVOTEE AND LIFE-BREATH JANGAMA*: the body is devotee and the life in the body is Jangama. Just as the devotee must serve Jangama so also the body should serve the life in it. By extension, the devotee should serve all mankind and all living beings. Serving mankind and life in general is thus the essence of the preaching of BASAVA.

7 *GANDHA PRASADA*: the sense object of smell, sanctified because it is dedicated to God.

8 *RASA PRASADA*: the sense object of taste, sanctified because it is dedicated to God.

9 *RUPA PRASADA*: the sense object of sight, sanctified because it is dedicated to God.

10 *SPARSA PRASADA*: the sense object of touch, sanctified because it is dedicated to God.

11 *SABDA PRASADA*: the sense object of sound, sanctified because it is dedicated to God.

12 *TRIPTI PRASADA*: contentment sanctified because it is dedicated God.

13 *KAYA PRASADA*: body sanctified because it is dedicated to God.

14 *PRASANNA PRASADA*: mind sanctified because it is dedicated to God.

15 *PARAMANANDA PRASADA*: possessions sanctified because they are dedicated to Got.

16 *PRASADA*: prasada literally means tranquility, peace that passeth understanding.

17 *NISHKALA LINGA*: linga that is indivisible, purna.

18 *NISSUNYA LINGA*: linga subtler than nishkala linga

19 *NIRANJANA LINGA*: linga the subtlest.

8

1 *GURU-LINGA-JANGAMA IS HUSBAND*: The relationship between the devotee and the God Siva is the same as the relationship between a wife and husband. The wife has to be devoted to the husband, and the husband to protect the wife.

Thus the devotee loves Siva and Siva protects the devotee. Since Siva comprises guru, linga and jangama, the trinity stands in the position of a husband. So serving the trinity, guru-linga-jangama, is serving Siva, the husband.

2 *SIX-STAGE BHAKTI*: The devotion of the devotee should pass through six stages in order to attain perfection. They are (1) *Sraddha* (diligence), (2) *Nishtha* (unwaveringness), (3) *Avadhana* (intentness), (4), *Anubhava* (enlightenment), (5) *Ananda* (beatitude), (6) *Samasara* (absoluteness.

3 *EIGHT-FOLD FORT (ASHTAVARANA)*: (1) Sacred ash that is smeared all over the body is *Bhasma*, (2) the sacred nut worn on the various parts of the body is *Rudraksha*, (3) sacred formula of siva's name chanted is *Mantra*, (4) the religious teacher is *Guru*, (5) the sign of god worn on the body is *Linga*, (6) the saiva saint to be served by the devotee is *Jangama*, (7) the water sanctified by washing of the feet of Guru-Linga-Jangama is *Padodaka*, (8) and the food presented by Guru-Linga-Jangama to the devotee is Prasada. These eight objects are like eight walls of a fortress to protect the devotee against all forces of evil.

4 *FIVE-FOLD CONDUCT (PANCACARA)*: Five rules of conduct are prescribed for a devotee: (1) wearing a linga on the body is *Lingacara*, (2) being pure in daily activities is *Sadacara*, (3) striving hard for the establishment of the order of saivism is *Sivacara*, (4) being dutiful and responsible to the team of saiva devotees is *Gana cara*, (5) and serving the devotees with humility is *Bhrityacara*.

5 *NINE DOORS OF THE BODY*: Five organs of sense (nose, tongue, eye, ear and skin) together with the personal god (ishta linga) worn on the body, the subtle form of linga (prana linga) worn on the inner body and the subtlest form of linga (Bhava Linga) worn on the innermost part of the body are the nine gate ways of the body where nine lingas are installed passing through which the experiences of the devotee are purged of their baseness. The nine lingas are respectively: (1) *Acara Linga*, (2) *Guru Linga*, (3) *Siva Linga*, (4) *Jangama Linga*, (5) *Prasada Linga*, (6) *Mahalinga*, (7) *Nishkala Linga*, (8) *Nissunya Linga*, and (9) *Nranjana Linga*. These nine lingas are nothing but divine motivations of the devotee personified as nine aspects of God.

9

1 *SARANA*: a devotee who has progressed in the path of God in such a way as to set an example to the initiates.

2 *SIVA BHAKTA*: a devotee of god Siva.

3 *BENARES*: a place of pilgrimage of the Hindus.

4 *KAILAS*: a peak of Himalayas where Siva is said to be residing. A place of pilgrimage of the Hindus.

5 *SADACARA*: See 8-4.

10

1 *DASOHI*: a devotee who observes dasoha in its strictest sense. See 1-1.

2 *PERFECTED DASOHI*: termed as Arudha Dasohi in the text.

11

1 *BHAKTA-MAHESWARA-PRASADI-PRANALINGI-SARANA-AIKYA*: are the six stages of the devotee in the path of perfection. See 8-2.

2 *SARANA SPOUSE AND LINGA HUSBAND*: See 8-1.

12

1 *LINGACARA-SADACARA-SIVACARA-GANACARA-BHARITYACARA*: See 8-4.

13

1 *SIVA-VISHNU*: The two prominent gods still worshipped by Hindus. The worshippers of Siva generally do not worship Vishnu and likewise Vishnu worshippers generally do not worship Siva.

2 *BASADI-VASATI*: Jaina temple. Vasati in Sanskrit means a dwelling place.

3 *VIHARA*: BOUDDHA TEMPLE, originally a hall where the monks meet or walked about; afterwards these halls were used as temples.

4 *PRANA JANGAMA*: the life breath that resides in any living creature.

14

1 *NAMASKAR*: A word of greeting like "Good Morning". The word namaskara literally means "act of bowing" before a person to show respect.

2 *DARSANA*: Holy vision.

15

1 *MOTHER IS GOD.....*: These lines are from Taittiriyopanishad.

16

1 *WORLDLY MAN*: a man who goes through the cycle of birth and death and has no spiritual craving.

2 *ILLUSTRIOUS HOUSE*: Mahamane in the text; a house where a devotee dwells.